To: The Poultons
Best Wishes,

BUSHWHACKED at the FLORA-BAMA

Copyright 2012
Wagon Publishing
Chris E. Warner

By Chris Warner
With Joe Gilchrist
Find the Author on Facebook:
Christopher Edward Warner
or Twitter @Cdubayou

Cover, inside pictures and logo courtesy of
Ken Cooper of the Orange Beach Community Website (OBA)
and the Flora-Bama

Layout, design and inside jacket photos
by Jamie Welch *www.jamie-welch.com*

ISBN# 978-0-9796284-4-3

Dedicated to the Flora-Bama Players.

"*Music is the balm that heals the forlorn ache of a distant star.*"
-Don Williams, Jr

Contents

Preface 3

Introduction 14

Chapter One – *"Bushwhacked"* 18

Chapter Two – *"Getting to Know Joe"* 30

Chapter Three – *"Ivan the Terrible"* 42

Chapter Four – *"Pleasure Island"* 46

Chapter Five – *"Getting Started"* 51

Chapter Six – *"Laughter and Song"* 64

Chapter Seven – *"Beach Polluter (BP)"* 74

Chapter Eight – *"The Mullet Toss"* 98

Chapter Nine – *"The Nashville Connection"* 106

Chapter Ten – *"Music to the Rescue"* 122

Chapter Eleven – *"Mr. Frank Brown"* 131

Chapter Twelve – *"Having Fun: The Principle Business of Life"* 137

Chapter Thirteen – *"Patriotism"* 143

Chapter Fourteen – *"The Rise and Decline of the Redneck Riviera"* .. 147

Chapter Fifteen – *"The Polar Bear Dip"* 152

Chapter Sixteen – *"An Analysis of Integrity of our Current Class of American Political Leadership"* 158

Chapter Seventeen – *"The Future of the Flora-Bama"* 164

Epilogue 167

Afterword with Joe Gilchrist 170

Bibliography 175

Preface

Lower Alabama, or "L.A." as it is often affectionately called in adjacent parts of Northwest Florida, is a particularly colorful, wholly remarkable, visually spectacular place—one certainly deserving of the sometimes reviled, often revered "Redneck Riviera" moniker. Nearby, the sleepy Port City of Mobile, Alabama's settlers are largely given credit for bringing Mardi Gras zaniness to the North American Continent; although the good Cajun French folks of Louisiana, with their unquenchable joie de vivre and their undeniable mantra "Laissez-les bon temps roulez," claim to have perfected it. Regardless, reveling, recreation-minded Southerners from the Pelican State to Georgia, Tennessee, Kentucky and Arkansas all eventually find their way to the Deep South's traditional, favored beach vacation playground.

The Redneck Riviera is a foamy, gritty strip of surf and sand that stretches over 100 miles from the State of Mississippi all the way along Alabama and Florida's scenic rural Highway 98. Sometimes referred to as the Azalea Coast, it is arguably home of the world's most beautiful beaches—sugar white grains of sand, gently washed by a rolling azure sea, and home also to the country's best spring breaks, amidst wacky water fun parks for the kids, body art tattoo parlors, cold draft beer joints, boiled blue crab shacks, homemade hamburger barns, cheap tee shirt boutiques and a devout overabundance of tourist trash and trinket shops.

The Redneck Riviera boasts high-rise condominiums with beautiful, buzzed, skinny, country girls on every air-conditioned floor. Further, the Mullet Toss behind the oversized brassiere-strewn Flora-Bama—that annual rite of passage for all Southern 21-year olds, makes tailgating at a NASCAR infield appear "hoity-toity." The always-heavy beach traffic for the annual April bare-bodied beach festivities on The Line is a healthy Southern parade of half-jacked pick-up trucks, pimped-out muscle cars, Harley-Davidson motorcycles, convertible Corvettes, Mercedes Benz, over-sized gas-guzzling Hummers, SUV's and Beamers. Perhaps that's the irresistible charm of the Redneck Riviera—it's so darn funky, it's always fun!

From Memorial Day to Labor Day the Deep South traditionally vacations here. Southerners from Louisiana to Georgia and beyond to the former Mason-Dixon Line have invested millions in its continuing condominium and commercial growth and development, branding it with a certain undeniably Southern, and particularly Bohemian flair. Paint the loveable, iconic Flora-Bama, the last of the Great American Road Houses, as an integral part of this modern gulf coastal canvas of recreation, rest and relaxation.

An avowed holdout from high property taxes and fleeting American freedoms, the adorable Flora-Bama provides a steady stream of unadulterated, reveling relief to loyal local members and curious, fun-seeking tourists from around the world. Described as the quintessential beach bar, the Flora-Bama's global reputation now proudly includes the moniker of "Hurricane Ivan Survivor."

"We call The Flora-Bama our five-star roadhouse," said Bebe Gauntt, spokesperson for the Alabama Gulf Coast Convention and Visitor's Bureau. "You can find something going on there anytime day or night. You might even walk in on a wedding." And many have.

Chuck Geiss, Publisher of the popular Birmingham, Alabama community-based newspaper *Black & White*, wrote glowingly of the tackily unrefined Flora-Bama in a post-Hurricane Ivan (September 2004) editorial, that the ephemeral Pumphouse's pre-Ivan layout forced confused revelers to enter through an unusually tiny package store, and that there was a constant jam of musicians singing.

> "…of honky-tonks, whiskey and love won and lost. Automobiles and motorcycles in the parking lot often foreshadowed the odd mix of patrons inside, usually a collection of hard-drinking locals, bikers, Navy flyboys, well-oiled tourists, rowdy college kids, and always a thirsty Canadian or two."

Born again Christians don't normally like live music, singing and dancing because it's just too close to fornicating. However, an innocent visit to the Flora-Bama is a must for anyone compiling or completing a serious bucket list. Whether it is the ideal beach location, the daily live music, the lovely visuals or the tasty, ice cold adult beverages regularly served, something intrinsically special continues to keep people coming back to the country's most unique outdoor lounge and package store.

In John Grisham's blockbuster novel, *The Firm*, which was later made into a movie by the same title starring actor Tom Cruise, the Flora-Bama fittingly served as a charming Southern oasis, a veritable passport to chill or thrill, for embattled protagonist Mitch McDeere, who had to get himself a cold one at the Flora-Bama.

While growing up in nearby Foley, Alabama, Crimson Tide and Oakland Raider quarterback-to-be, Kenny Stabler, once quoted as saying that "There's nothing wrong with studying your plays by the light of the jukebox," was at one time a noted regular at *The Line*. Island Escapist and Chief Parrothead Jimmy Buffet, of nearby Fairhope, was also an occasional patron, after he became eternally "Wasted away again in Margaritaville." Joe said that Kenny Stabler gets the credit for introducing Jimmy to Joe during the Flora-Bama's early days.

Homegrown *American Idol* Taylor Hicks of Birmingham, Alabama, according to legend, as a boy, dreamed of playing the stages of the Flora-Bama, and did so just before he made his memorable run toward eventual *Idol* fame. Of course, Taylor Hicks has been back to the Flora-Bama and played many times since. Reportedly, Alabama's avowed favorite son keeps a framed picture of the beloved beach bar straddling the state line where he got his start—by his bedside.

The celebrity visitor list at the Flora-Bama is considerable, and for good reason—it is simply *the place to be* on the Gulf Coast.

Alan Brockman, who produced "The Last Great American Roadhouse," the official documentary of the Flora-Bama (2006), understands that the Flora-Bama is a magnet for uniquely good times and great folks from all parts and walks of life.

> "Deep within the heart of Dixie lies something so real, so true, so roots, that only a fortunate number of us have had the blessing to come across in our lifetimes. How often can one find themselves sitting on a bar stool with one leg in Florida and one leg in Alabama? Meanwhile, the yuppie on your left is discussing Hank, while the Hell's Angel on your right is forecasting upcoming economic trends? It is surreal; the aura…an inescapable beauty of a time, a place and a lifestyle, that is often forgotten in modern society…the love, the leisure and the lifestyle…of the Flora-Bama."
>
> *- Alan Brockman, producer*

***

I met Joe Gilchrist through his brother, David, a Birmingham, Alabama-based stock broker. On a cold December morning in 2009, I gave a speech to the Shades Mountain Sunrise Rotary inside Birmingham's famed Vulcan Statue Museum. The nearby Vulcan Statue is the largest iron sculpture in the United States.

The talk I gave early that day was on the history of American college football in the South, which is a related section in my thrice-published book, "A

Tailgater's Guide to SEC Football." Toward the discussion's end I segued into the fascinating topic of the massive tragedy of Birmingham-based rehab giant HealthSouth's accounting fraud and its infamously sinister former CEO, Richard Scrushy, as I had recently written two books, *The Wagon to Disaster,* a tell-all by the former *CFO,* Aaron Beam, and *Professional Bone*, a novel, inspired by the same true story.

The somewhat lengthy address went well. I could tell by the audience's collective countenance and by their many questions that it was stimulating; and that's really all you can hope for on a chilly, winter morning. After the speech I shook a few hands, signed some books and made my way out of the museum, as I still had to drive four hours to the small city of Fairhope, in Lower Alabama, where I lived.

Joe's brother, David Gilchrist, approached me on my way to the parking lot. He had greeted me and bought a book only moments earlier, so I thought it was a bit odd for him to seek me. The temperature was below freezing and the wind whipped on Red Mountain. I was ready to get out of there. I wanted to get warm and to get home. Nevertheless, I was cordial.

David hastily told me that for more than twenty years he had been trying to get his brother to write a book, but to no avail. He explained his point of view.

"My brother Joe is an amazing guy. He is really something. He has lived five lifetimes! You just have to meet him. It might take him a while to get to know you, but I think you could be the one to help him get this done. You live down there and you are an experienced writer. If he doesn't do it, I'm afraid he's going to get sick one day and then it'll be too late," he said.

As a writer and author, people regularly approach me with book ideas. Having experience in publishing, I always cautiously remind everyone who speaks enthusiastically of this tightrope act—that there are ostensibly good book ideas and great book ideas, and that you need only pursue the great ones—as the world is full of mediocre books. I respectfully explained this to David.

He was undaunted. Like a polished salesman, he went back to talking excitedly about the book's undeniable, potential subject.

"My brother is different. He is just a fascinating guy, and there's a story there. You just have to meet him."

I gave up.

"Who is your brother?" I asked, knowing I was in for it.

"Joe Gilchrist. He owns the Flora-Bama. It's a place down on the gulf."

"I know where it is." I replied. My eyebrows rose simultaneously, along with the intonation of my voice, and I looked at him with unwavering interest. I'd experienced the Flora-Bama.

"I want to meet your brother." I answered, matter-of-factly.

David gleamed and seemed glad that I was interested. However, I could see in his eyes it still wasn't a sure thing. Telling stories never is. It wasn't like his brother was sitting around waiting for me to write his book. Nevertheless, he threw me off with what he said next.

"Now, you need to know that my brother is going through a difficult time. He's dealing with some personal matters right now, so it might be a while until he can do it or at least get started. You'll just have to meet him and see."

I was perplexed. "Well, what is it?" I asked.

"I can't talk about it, but you'll find out if you meet him and get to know him."

David grinned nonchalantly, as if the glowing, clandestine way in which he spoke of Joe was normal—and just part of his life as Joe Gilchrist's older brother.

I was a bit befuddled.

"Joe and I get together every holiday season. I'll tell him about you and after that you'll be able to get in touch with him."

Before departing David politely gave me his card and asked me to follow up with him after the holidays.

David explained that he and Joe always get together at the family's ranch in Troy, Alabama, where their extended relatives are from, and where they grew up. I later learned that they had recently lost their older brother, Lane Gilchrist, a former Mayor of Gulf Breeze, Florida, of thirty years; so the annual reunion was likely particularly somber and nostalgic for the two, given their loss.

Early in 2010, I followed up with David. As promised, over the following Christmas and New Year's break, David spoke to Joe about me. He said that I should send Joe a couple of my books and set up a meeting. I did exactly that.

I sent Joe the recommended books and an accompanying letter explaining that his brother had approached me about possibly helping him write a book about his amazing life as the Flora-Bama's adventurous, reveling proprietor. I didn't use those exact words, but I was as direct as I was respectful in my first correspondence with Joe. Soon after, I heard from him.

Joe asked me to meet him in late January on a weekday at 3:30 p.m. at the Silver Moon Lounge across from the Flora-Bama. This local favorite, at the time, was a classic, throwback haunt which also served as a Package Liquor Store and a veritable State of Florida Lottery ticket depot. The building it was in was actually an old Kentucky Fried Chicken joint replete with the remnants of an old drive through window that is still used to hustle bottled booze and cold beer. But "The Moon" was really all about the music. It was where some of the area and Nashville's best songwriting talent regularly played. That afternoon was no exception. Bo Roberts was performing live.

Like others before and after him, Bo Roberts moved to the coast to be a regular at the Flora-Bama and the Silver Moon after he visited from Nashville one summer. He and Joe quickly became close friends, and as their friendship grew, so did Joe's insatiable love and steadfast dedication toward the most forgotten man in the music business—the songwriter. Joe saw early that the songwriters were so important, but that they were as underappreciated as they were underpaid, despite their seemingly indispensable nature. Joe recognized their collective struggle and has worked for years to try and soften the plight of area singer-songwriters by hiring them to play at the Bama, by finding them a comfortable place to crash, or by getting his local friends in the restaurant and bar business to hire them for side gigs.

Texas-based recording artist Kim Carson, in between live music sets on the main Flora-Bama stage, aptly tagged Joe as "the Patron Saint of Song Writers." Joe's undying dedication to the songwriting craft has spawned the Frank Brown Songwriter's Festival that occurs every November at the Flora-Bama, named after Mr. Frank Brown, one of the Flora-Bama's earliest characters, and a person we will later discuss at length.

The constant entertainment allure of the Flora-Bama has a tremendous impact on area tourism. Local businesses benefit tremendously from beachgoers and partiers clamoring to "Do it on the Line." Hotels, restaurants, condominium rentals, convenience retailers and yes—even other bars, benefit from the Bama's far-reaching, collective draw. The ephemeral sand juke box and island getaway is an avowed economic force multiplier for the entire Alabama-

Florida gulf coast area, as it is a favored destination for visitors in the Southern proverbial know.

I did not realize it at the time, but Joe was predictably an hour late for our meeting. However, I was told at the bar to drink whatever I wanted—that it was on the house—until Joe arrived. I thought that was nice of him. I later learned that Joe rarely wears a watch and goes by what a casual observer would typify as "island time." Joe's pace is slow and steady. He rarely rushes; but he is nevertheless, always equally thorough.

Bo Roberts and his band, which included Willie Nelson's former guitarist, Jody Payne, were sounding really good, so I grabbed a cold beer and sat directly in front of them against the wall and enjoyed the show for nearly an entire set before Joe finally arrived.

Bo played a song that afternoon that I have remembered ever since and made one of my favorites. Like any memorable tune, Bo's song titled, "My Baby Makes my Day," tells a story. It's a picturesque account of how a woman lights candles in her bedroom and puts on a sexy negligee' while she is waiting for her man to come home from work. The song is cleverly worded, but it has a catchy tune and an undeniable effect, because it creates such simple imagery for the listener's perspective and enjoyment. It is always a popular request when Bo plays, evidenced by the fact it was recently bought and recorded by the label of rising country singer Crystal Shawanda. It is a part of Crystal's new album, released in February 2012, titled, "Just Like You."

Avid country and western fans will recognize one of Bo's more renowned penned songs, "Ten With a Two," which was made popular by recording artists Willie Nelson and Kenny Chesney. The punch line of the song is its undeniable title, "Last night I came home at two with a ten, but at ten I woke up with a two. I never been to bed with an ugly woman but I sure woke up with a few." Bo also hit number one back in 1983 with the tune, "You're Out Doing What I'm Here Doing Without," recorded by Gene Watson.

Joe Gilchrist is a portly fellow with a hearty smile, an open ear and an undeniable wit and charm. He has a loveable countenance and a wonderful penchant for laughter and listening patiently to others. He is a gracious person and believes wholeheartedly in showing others reverence and respect. Value-driven, Joe has made human dignity a centerpiece of his customer service philosophy at the Flora-Bama.

An inconspicuous fellow entered the bar and asked the bartender a question. The bartender looked to me and pointed. Somewhat to my surprise, I realized it was Joe.

Joe and I made eye contact. I stood and walked toward him at the bar. He met me halfway with an outreached right hand and a broad smile as captivating as his created place.

"Sorry I am a little late," he said, as we shook hands for the first time. "I was tending to a few things."

It was no matter to me, as I was digging the music and the complimentary suds. We talked a little, enjoyed another round and a couple more of Bo's great songs before Joe told me it was "time to go." There was a noticeable change in the tone and ring to his voice that made it sound important.

"Sure thing," I said, clueless as to where we were going.

We left the Silver Moon and jumped into Joe's early model, beat-up, slightly rusted and faded, Mardi Gras-bead-cluttered, red, four-by-four, Ford F-150 pickup truck and drove half a block to the bleached clam shell lot outside of his business office near the Florida and Alabama state lines. With subtle trepidation the sturdy 67-year old walked from the unseasonable, blustery cold into a cozy room of thirty or more anxious, waiting faces. To me, it felt like a setup. I could tell immediately something was going down.

The mood was somber. Barely a sound was heard. In earlier, carefree times, things weren't like this. Normally, everyone was bubbly and happy—loving life as usual in their dream jobs working at one of the country's coolest hot spots. However, on this day, things were much different; and everyone in attendance knew it.

Present were Joe's most trusted and respected employees—a privileged group of faithful workers who had been with the company for several or more years. Each of the particularly seasoned crew held generous dividend-paying stock in the Flora-Bama, as well as health care benefits, quite the anomaly for bar employees anywhere.

Each shareholder focused intently on the man they admired and respected—and who made their world so fun and comfortable. Having earlier caught wind of the impending announcement, they braced themselves for the inevitable. This, they knew, would be difficult. Unfortunately, on this occasion, they had no choice but to deal with it.

Dressed in his regular attire of softly wrinkled slacks, a collared shirt, a wind breaker and beat-up, loosely-tied white tennis shoes, Gilchrist addressed the people that for years had made it all possible. The words came deliberately, as if he were struggling to articulate; to get it over with. As he began to speak, you could have heard a mouse peeing on cotton.

"Many of you have heard that I have been having financial difficulties. This is true. But, what I want you all to know is that this is not your fault. I brought these circumstances upon myself because of investment decisions *I* have made. *You* had nothing to do with this. This is not because of *you*."

Taking the tenor of a father talking to his children, Gilchrist's eyes reddened and his speech slowed. By the hardest, he continued.

"Unfortunately, I invested most of my personal wealth in the highly speculative real estate market, and I'm upside down. The properties I own are worth a third of what I paid for them and there's no end in sight. I have no choice but to file for bankruptcy."

The bitter news fell hard on the ears of his downtrodden troops. Their pale, expressionless faces reflected their worst fears. However, Joe tried his best to find a silver lining amidst a growing cloud of doubt, to provide hope in an otherwise somber moment.

"The good news is that we are pretty sure the Flora-Bama and the Silver Moon (package liquor store and lounge across the street) are safe. They are profitable. They and you are not going to suffer because of this, and that's the way it should be, because you guys have made it all possible. We have assembled a great team of bankruptcy lawyers and we feel we are going to be able to survive this. We'll just have to wait and see."

Gilchrist composed himself and segued into another important topic—the long-overdue Flora-Bama rebuilding project—the one everyone had been waiting on for nearly six years. In September, 2004, when Hurricane Ivan, a Category Four storm, scored a direct hit on the bar, its massive tidal surge ripped through the revered hodge-podge of outdoor bars, Southeastern Conference banner flags, oversized wooden spools, plywood bathrooms and makeshift dance floors, leaving it a shell of its former inglorious self.

Hurricane Ivan was the tenth-most intense Atlantic hurricane ever recorded. Ivan formed as a Cape Verde-type cyclone in early September and became the season's ninth named storm and the fourth major hurricane of the year. It even reached Category Five strength on the Saffir-Simpson Hurricane Scale, the strongest possible category. At its destructive zenith, in the center of the Gulf of Mexico, Ivan was the size of the great State of Texas. Furthermore, it spawned 117 tornadoes across the eastern United States.

Within hours after the powerful hurricane made a most violent landfall, it was reported on CNN, FOX and other national news outlets that the Flora-Bama was "no longer," and "had been washed completely away" in the fast-rising, tidal flood waters. Over the following difficult days, the Alabama Gulf Coast Convention & Visitors Bureau was deluged with over 5,000 phone calls from every corner of the country and the world, from people wanting to know if it was really true—that "…the revered Flora-Bama was no longer?"

**

Gilchrist perked up, and spoke hopefully of the future. "The good news is that we are progressing with the rebuild of the Flora-Bama. It will be done in stages, and it is going to take time, but we're going to rebuild. We've had trouble with the local government around here in getting the proper permits to do what we can and cannot do, but we think that's behind us now. We think we're finally ready to move forward."

At this time a large crane could be seen inside the Flora-Bama compound, waiting to drive tall, thick, chemically-treated wooden pylons—former tall, sturdy trees—tens of feet into the white powder sand. Photocopies of the newly-completed renovation plans distributed to the employees called for a multi-story venue replete with an elevator and new set of indoor bathrooms. The blueprints were impressive and were a full glimpse of what could be—of what used to be—before Ivan disrupted a phenomenal beach party that had carried on unabated for years.

Since Hurricane Ivan, the Bama had never really been the same as it once was. It had lost much of its original building and overall structure to the point where it was really a different place, as it was no longer able to accommodate as many in the same artful manner it once did. Many of the old-timers and regulars still lamented this painful fact. They pined for a return to the Bama's glory years, a magical time etched firmly into their fading memory banks; a time that was forever part of what made them whole.

The meeting was buoyed by co-owner Pat McClellan's thoughtful gift of several hot, delivered pizzas, but it was nonetheless sobering overall, as Joe's formal announcement was the stark revelation that his bankruptcy could be the beginning of a shuttering end to the revered institution known as the Flora-Bama. It was a chilling acknowledgment, and an absolute monster buzz kill to the Bama stockholding employees in attendance.

In retrospect, Joe was not confident in speech that he would not lose the Flora-Bama. He only said he was "pretty sure" that the Bama would survive; but he finished with the telling caveat, "We'll have to see," and it was those unsure words that would ultimately prove to be most moving, and concerning.

It was clear that these were tough financial times—some of the toughest the country had seen in many years. Joe Gilchrist, the former multi-millionaire, the ultra-entrepreneur, the guy who had milked the American Dream for seemingly all it was possibly worth—was living proof of the sheer breadth and depth of the economic crash that had unmercifully befallen the United States of America. The revelation was as sobering as it was a harbinger of doubt about the country's future. If Joe Gilchrist, the owner of the Flora-Bama, had to file for bankruptcy, "What's in store for the rest of us?" was all I could think. I shuddered.

Introduction

By January 2010 the U.S. economy was still feeling the reeling effects of one of the worst recessions in recorded history. A confluence of the bursting of the stock market and real estate bubbles, coupled with the debilitating, confidence-shattering corporate fraud and greed problem, made for tough economic times worldwide. The stock market, which had peaked at 14,168 (DJI) on October 9, 2007, was clamoring to climb back to a respectable level of around 10,000, having hit a nadir of 6,500 just months earlier.

This financial funk was punctuated by distrusting, billionaire charlatans like HealthSouth's Richard Scrushy and Ponzi scheme rip-off artists Bernie Madoff and Allen Stanford, among others. American capitalism was on the proverbial ropes. A voting public so disgusted with the government status quo fifteen months earlier elected the country's first black president—an inexperienced, former leftist radical with dubious citizenship credentials who some claimed was the chosen Manchurian Candidate, backed by an elite, international machine bent on destroying the United State's global hegemony.

All of which were signs that the U.S. citizens were barreling down an increasingly steeper, socialistic path—but only because their single, unconscionable alternative was four more years of hollow Republican rule. Party realignment, like a slow and heavy pendulum, had finally made its predictable swing, bringing with it the "hope and change" mantra that inspired millions in the North and South to vote Democratic for the first time.

Nevertheless, Alabama was a skeptical holdout, voting instead for Arizona's United States Senator, John McCain. This was unlike its neighbor Florida, which tipped in favor of the new President. However, despite the recent political shift, the nation's economy faltered nonetheless. The dismal economy of George Bush Junior's last year in the White House continued into his successor's presidency. Where there was once hope, there was only despair; and where there was once change, there was apparently none to spare. People everywhere were either going broke or were already destitute. Draining one's halved 401k became the unfortunate, mandatory rule, rather than the unthinkable exception for many.

Even the Redneck Riviera, that dreamy strip of turquoise and talc that graces the Gulf Shores area from Fort Morgan to Perdido Key and beyond; the island getaway that for several years had enjoyed a continued seasonal bounty of tourist dollars—could not avoid the wrath of the violent financial typhoon that rocked American, and world markets to their collective cores.

Because of this unforeseen money malady, condominium rentals were way down, as were every other sales tally associated with healthy beach tourism. Restaurants, bars, grocery stores, gas stations, retail shops and a host of other small area businesses had all benefited from the trickle-down reality of the former long-standing bull market. This particularly cold and bearish winter, however, was not one of these times. People were hurting. Beach vacations were considered a luxury far more elusive than a steady paycheck.

***

In February 2010, I had been living alone for six months, separated from my wife of 12 years and daughters ages ten and seven, and my dog. My marriage, like so many others, it seemed, didn't go as planned. The last five years had been particularly unhappy. While the prospect of divorce was nearly as scary to me as it certainly was for my two young children, it was necessary. Further, it meant I was essentially starting over towards being happy. For too long I had only existed. I was ready to start living again. Little did I know, my life was about to change irrevocably toward that purposeful end.

I grew up in South Louisiana's mysterious Cajun Country, in New Iberia, the Iberia Parish Seat. I attended Louisiana State University in Baton Rouge on academic scholarship. Through diligence I received two degrees from the Ole War Skule, and a few years later, a doctorate from the University of New Orleans. At 40, I had worked as a bureaucrat, a college professor, a gifted high school teacher, a radio and television talk show host and a writer and author, having written and published a dozen different titles. I'd developed a knack for capturing likeness through words and more importantly—for telling tales about interesting people and the things they've done—or failed to do. In doing so, I learned the great human importance and infinite power of well-told stories.

I vaguely recall at some point during my young adulthood visiting the Flora-Bama while vacationing on the Alabama coast. I remembered it as a fun place—as *the* place to party and have a good time at the beach. Nevertheless, in hindsight, I really knew nothing about it.

***

After Joe's meeting at the Flora-Bama offices, he and I got back into his beat-up red Ford pickup. The air was already chilly, the sun a recent memory, the orange ball having earlier ducked below the glowing western sky. The wind still whipped. When we were both back inside the warmer vehicle confines, I saw the emotion in his countenance. What he had done was difficult. I likened it to a situation I had recently endured. I could wholeheartedly relate.

I broke the silence.

"Joe, my wife and I just separated. The toughest thing was telling our kids. What you just did reminded me of when we sat down and told them. Like you, I told them it was not their fault; and I think that was important." Joe empathically looked to me in a way that told me he understood.

I paused, and continued. "It still wasn't easy."

Joe nodded his head and looked away momentarily.

He refrained from turning the engine. We just sat there together, in cold silence.

He stared in yet a different direction and then turned back to me.

"How long were you married?" he asked.

"Twelve years almost," I answered.

"I'm sorry," Joe offered. "I know how difficult that can be. I went through it."

I sort of shrugged and nodded a thank you, not wanting to acknowledge the pain I was going through; but he recognized it.

"Well, I didn't see that coming," I said, gesturing back into the office, trying to communicate to him how shocked I was at the announcement. After all, we had just met.

Joe looked at me with puppy dog eyes and managed, "I thought it might be a good way to start the book."

And so it went.

***

This book explains the amazing story of how an American dream became an unbelievable reality, birthing a legend in the process. I spent two years closely following the actions of Joe Gilchrist, originator of the legendary Flora-Bama Lounge, Oyster Bar & Package Store. The place, molded in the spirit of its remarkable creator, is a stunning, Southern innovation of good times for great people. But like so many other wonderful things that have been great and have seemingly run their exhaustible, mortal course, it too—the revered Flora-Bama—like the embattled United States of America, is vulnerable to inevitable collapse.

This book is about a different way, or approach to living life, in one of the prettiest places in North America—Lower Alabama and Northwest Florida—the revered, but often misunderstood, "Redneck Riviera."

This book is about how quickly things in our country are changing, and for the apparent worst. Freedoms and liberties our forefathers died for are slowly being eroded by an apathetic public and an overbearing, self-serving and unaccountable government bent on controlling nearly every aspect of our lives.

America was once the land of the free, the home of the brave—an entrepreneur's dream. Today, the things we hold dear and revere as free, enterprising Americans—our way of life—hangs seemingly in the balance.

Hopefully this book will inspire not just Southerners, but all Americans who think and feel, to act accordingly, individually and collectively to change the current dismal course of events, so that the most cherished aspects of our unprecedented American experiment—what makes us truly American—are not forever, regrettably lost.

And finally, this book is about the larger journey of life, that burning desire within us all to find peace, love, happiness and contentment; before we die.

Chapter One

Bushwhacked

"He was subject to a kind of disease,
which at that time they called lack of money."

-Francois Rabelais

The Flora-Bama is a massive, sprawling wooden, twined, vinyl labyrinth that hugs the common border of Florida and Alabama running to the gulf's foamy edge. There you will regularly find every imaginable class of Southerner—and some utterly classless—jammed into the various nooks, crannies and satellite bars scattered throughout the roadside compound. There is live music all day long and usually until early morning in the summer; lots of gulf seafood, and of course, plenty of trademark, frothy bushwhackers, refreshing cocktails and ice cold beer served in recyclable aluminum cans.

Architecturally the place is a notable blend of Southern Redneck Beach Construction and Circus Tent. Once you traverse through the salted tarp and fashioned moldings made of twisted white PVC pipe and pylon driftwood, you are met by a marriage of old, mildewing wedding tents held together by tethered ropes, rusty chains and several splintered layers of marine plywood in various states of warp and decay. One could easily get the impression that they never really cleaned up after the many hurricanes that have hit here—that they have just built around the violent mess to keep the party going—and that is partly true.

The whole place exudes a youthful, weekend, tree house-like quality and it's a near miracle that the fabled landmark still stands. Black Sharpie Pen writing is welcomed and encouraged on the plywood walls. Port-o-potties are the answer for fetid bathroom facilities, and the faint, redolent odor of shucked oysters and stale draft beer lingers everywhere, like the many various and sundry women's bras that hang along taut lines ran amongst the rafters, undoubtedly an ephemeral reminder of the nether-worldly, strictly adult business at hand that happens regularly here.

Drawn to this place are some of the best singer-songwriters and modern country/rock bands you will ever see at a bar, some of the most attractive women you'll ever eyeball anywhere, and some of the most far-out bikers, tripped-out truckers, good ole' boys, roadies, hippies, hipsters, nerds, bros, country club members, fats, frats, skinnies, rich, poor and plain old folks from all over the place. You will routinely see old ladies in bright funny hats, rail thin River Delta bachelorettes, bloated working alcoholics, Navy service people and Marines, people you knew, people you could've probably known, people you would otherwise never see "out" in a million years...except at the world-famous, one-and-only, Flora-Bama. It is quite possibly the best darn bar you've ever enjoyed—if you have ever been lucky enough to go there.

***

I once read in a *USA Today* poll that most people who have money admit to deriving more pleasure in giving it to others than they do spending it on themselves. Joe Gilchrist is certainly one of these people. In the short time I've known him since his bankruptcy I have repeatedly seen him give to others in need until it hurts. He is no longer independently wealthy like he once was when times weren't so tough. Nevertheless, he still gives, and because of that, I like to call him "Deep Pockets."

Joe explained to me that in his role as owner and general manager of the Flora-Bama he was always in a unique position to help many people, and that he always relished the opportunity to do so. He told me that up until recently he had made a good bit of money buying and selling and renting real estate, and that he felt he could continue to do so for as long as he wanted. That was obviously *before* the stock and real estate markets simultaneously crashed in 2008.

When the economy was riding high, there was no shortage of successful real estate agents in the Perdido Key and Orange Beach areas. Further, most of them frequented the Flora-Bama. Joe said that he invested in many different types of speculative real estate ventures—condominiums, apartment complexes, commercial and residential land parcels, and even plotted residential subdivisions, hoping to eventually parlay his ongoing real estate success into even more money, so that he could in turn—"help more people." However, ironically, in the end, it turned out to be Joe who needed help to pay bad debts, the back taxes he owed the federal government, and to save his beloved, one-of-a-kind roadhouse, the Flora-Bama.

The term "bushwhacked" is the simple past tense and past participle of the verb "bushwhack." It has more than one meaning. In Joe's case, being bushwhacked implies that he was ambushed by an unforeseen foe—that he was the most unfortunate victim of a surprise attack. He didn't see it coming. Nobody did.

Joe told me he wholly trusted the tried and tested American investment institutions of the real estate and stock markets. It was and is, after all, where most wealthy people invest their money. Further, it was where many former wealthy Americans lost most of their accumulated assets during the latest financial correction.

Moreover, "bushwhacked" is the light-headed, easy feeling one derives after imbibing several frothy bushwhackers at the Flora-Bama; making the term the perfect double entendre example.

The bushwhacker drink is the Flora-Bama's trademark specialty adult beverage. A reported multiple spiced, frozen rum mixture of milk, cream of coconut, ice cream and Kahlua (there are other secret, delectable ingredients), the bushwhacker packs a powerful punch that sneaks up on you disguised as a milk shake. Bushwhackers are as strong as they are tasty—and they are quite delicious. When visiting the Flora-Bama, I highly recommend that you designate a driver and have a couple; and that you relax and allow yourself to enjoy the music, the characters, the panorama and the many available laughs.

Joe, like most Americans, certainly never imagined the economic Armageddon that descended upon the country in 2008. He admitted as much. Nevertheless, his bankruptcy and bleak personal financial situation resulting from the great recession placed many new challenges in his path. At age 67, when most people his age were anxiously anticipating retirement and their golden years, he was instead faced with a new, massive set of monetary hurdles to overcome. Ironically, like he was precariously some thirty-one years prior when he purchased the Flora-Bama—he had another long, arduous road ahead of him.

***

After his big, unexpected bankruptcy announcement, Joe invited me that same evening to a different local watering hole, Tipsea's, in Gulf Shores, Alabama, that also showcases live local musical and songwriting talent. Joe brought along a girlfriend that evening, Sandy Laird.

Sandy, like so many others singer/songwriter types before her, came to the Perdido Key area via Nashville, Tennessee. A pretty, blue-eyed blonde with a summer smile, Sandy made it to the beach as a youngster back in the mid 1990's, just as things were really taking shape for Joe and Pat McClellan, his eventual partner, and the Flora-Bama.

Sandy was friends with noted, Hall-of-Fame singer-songwriter Mickey Newbury, whom she met in Nashville. Famed country music legend Marty Robbins helped Sandy get to The Music City via her home state of Pennsylvania years before, in the process introducing her to some of the city's most inspiring musical talent and management.

Sandy recalled, "Marty Robbins helped me cut my first record in Nashville. He represented me and got me gigs. Mickey (Newbury) visited the Flora-Bama first. He came back to Nashville and told me all about it. It sounded great, and I came down with him shortly thereafter. I haven't left since, but for occasional road trips."

She paused for effect.

"I tell everybody all the time that I started at the top and have been working my way down ever since," she joked.

It was late January. The 2010 winter was unseasonably cold. Everyone in the area commented on how chilly it seemed compared to the winters of recent years past. The whimsical sun seemed to hardly ever break through the daytime clouds and the unforgiving wind blew incessantly, robbing your body of any trapped, latent heat. It was an uncomfortable time.

Despite the unfriendly beach resort weather, a few days earlier, just a week after the annual zany "Polar Bear Dip" at the Flora-Bama, where New Year's Day revelers wade faithfully into the icy gulf waters while before, during and afterward enjoying adult beverages, the University of Alabama football team—the revered Crimson Tide, on January 7, 2010, defeated the University of Texas Longhorns in the Rose Bowl in Pasadena, California to claim the undisputed Bowl Championship Series Collegiate Football National Championship. This was colossal news in Alabama, where winning football is typically more important than dry powder and potable water. More than half the state was in ecstasy.

Exactly a month later, on February 7, 2010, the New Orleans Saints, the theretofore perennial NFL doormat, in a monumental upset, defeated New Orleans native, University of Tennessee alumnus and NFL-All Pro Quarterback Peyton Manning, and the Indianapolis Colts, in Super Bowl XLIV in Miami's Sun Life Stadium.

The Rose Bowl victory was Alabama's first national championship in football since 1992. Coach Nick Saban, who became the first American college football coach to win national championships at two different schools (LSU in 2003), achieved in his third year in Tuscaloosa what Gene Stallings had accomplished 18 years prior—he returned pigskin glory to the beloved Capstone. Furthermore, it meant the Crimson Tide was better than their nemesis, the Auburn Tigers—Joe's alma mater—which gave them full reign in the State of Alabama—and that's a really big deal in these Southern parts, where football is a religion and Saturday is the sacred Sabbath.

In the upset victory over the Indianapolis Colts, New Orleans Saints Head Coach Sean Payton accomplished something that no man before him had—he led the formerly haphazard Saints to claim the biggest prize in football. Football fans everywhere in Lower Alabama and Northwest Florida were beside themselves. The stars had magically aligned. In a rare confluence of victorious football, braggin' rights—*in college and pro*—were firmly theirs.

Amazingly, Alabama's arch-nemesis, the Auburn Tigers, went on to win the 2011 BCS National Championship against Oregon, followed again by Alabama in 2012 (over LSU), meaning the BCS title remained in the State of Alabama for an unprecedented, three straight years.

That night at Tipsea's, a couple of local entertainers were hard at work having fun on the standing microphones. Rhonda Hart played her guitar and sang, along with her friend and colleague, the equally funny and talented, Elaine Petty.

Rhonda Hart is a singer/songwriter who co-authored the single "Did I shave my legs for this?" made famous by Deana Carter's 1996 debut album titled by the same name. A self-proclaimed cowgirl who grew up cowboyin' on a farm in Oregon, Rhonda, a raven-haired dynamo, is one of those larger than life characters who always seem to be going a mile-a-minute. She is also an attractive goof who loves to joke around and get crazy while she performs. Rhonda is a regular of the local entertainment scene, playing often with Elaine Petty, as "The Honky-Tonk Angels" or shaking a tambourine with Johnny

Barbados' band, "The Lucky Doggs," featuring the accomplished guitar of Luther Wamble, a Slidell, Louisiana native, who is a fine artist and one of the better technical guitar players I have heard. Luther can blaze.

Elaine Petty is another singer/songwriter of the same genre who has forged a reputation as a solid entertainer and a bona fide community favorite. Like most if not all of the local performers, she plays several area gigs every week, as a living on performing live music cannot be made at the Flora-Bama alone. Most of the area musicians hustle for their money. They must.

Joe explained to me that night in between songs that he not only hires the local talent to play at the Flora-Bama and the Silver Moon, but that he has always tried as often as he could to go and see them play at other area proprietorships to "support the cause," as he put it. Joe was clear early on that he was a staunch advocate of the area's many singer/songwriters, making me understand that they were the ones—the rhythm makers of the island—that helped the area become so unique and enjoyable to countless tourists and visitors.

Joe surprised me later that night when he told me he wanted me to stay as his guest for a few days in his luxury condominium, the penthouse atop the Phoenix Ten high-rise next door to the Flora-Bama, just inside the Alabama State Line. The place has a spectacular view, towering directly over the sparkling turquoise Gulf of Mexico—and the raucous Flora-Bama. He said he already had a few other guests staying there—migrant musicians and songwriters who welcomed the warm place to hang out and crash during the offseason. But, he said no one was staying in his master suite, so it was available.

At the time I was not working a nine-to-five job. I was writing and publishing books for multiple clients, teaching part-time and was basically working for myself. This gave me the free time I needed to take full advantage of an offer like Joe's. I was excited. I thanked him and told him I looked forward to meeting and spending some time with him and his creative friends.

Joe gave me the key to the penthouse and he and Sandy walked me up. He showed me into the unit and introduced me to Mike Bowland, an affable piano player and singer, who was hanging out in the living room area of the spacious condominium. We made quick company.

A former long-time denizen of Nashville's music scene, Mike Boland came to the Bama via Memphis in his early model motor home. He was looking for work playing his keyboard and crooning. Mike told the story that he got to Jackson, Mississippi and flipped a coin. He said that if it landed tails he was going to head to New Orleans and if it was heads he was going to venture to the Florida Keys. He has still never made it to the Keys, but he did head in that general, easterly direction, which brought him to the Flora-Bama.

Mike said that while on his way to the Keys, he was getting gas in Mobile, Alabama, when a random someone told him about the legendary Flora-Bama. He said his interest was immediately piqued and he got general directions as to where it was on the coast. Eventually, he said, he "blew right by the place."

"I thought it was a flea market," Mike recalled of the iconic road house straddling the Alabama Florida state lines.

Mike and his RV landed a mile or so east past the Florida State line at a campground. He asked the friendly proprietor where the place was that they "played all the live music." The man jumped into his vehicle and led Mike back directly the way he came down the beach highway to the dimly-lit Silver Moon, which at the time doubled as a package liquor store and popular listening room, where live music could be regularly heard. Soon after he met Joe Gilchrist and performed an impromptu concert. Joe hired Mike on the spot and he's been playing there seasonally ever since.

After Joe and Sandy made their way home for the night, Mike's son, Johnny Holiday, showed up in tow with what looked to be a twenty-something starlet—a strikingly beautiful redhead. They made quite the rosy couple on a cold winter's eve.

"The Bama's rocking!" announced an animated, pompadour-wearing Johnny, arm-in-arm with the smiling young lady. The bass from the drums played inside the Flora-Bama reverberated through the condominium—all the way to the Penthouse. We felt the drum beat from way up there.

Johnny Holiday was his stage name, I learned. Turned out that Mike's son was a multi-talented singer/songwriter, screen writer, actor and producer. More specifically, he was the guy who played Carl Perkins in Johnny Cash's depicted life in the motion picture "Walk the Line" with Joaquin Phoenix and Reese Witherspoon. Coincidentally, Jody Payne's son, Waylon, also had a role in the same film—playing Louisiana legend Jerry Lee Lewis.

I liked Johnny. He was extremely charismatic, easy-going and funny, as he loved to poke fun at his old man—Mike Bowland. The father-and-son duo constantly badgered and teased one another in my presence. In between gests they even collaborated on a song writing endeavor while I was there. I remember it had a great first line that gave you a full glimpse of the story. It went:

"I found out about her and him…best of luck to the both of them."

I don't recall if Johnny and his dad ever finished that song—but they should have—and sold it. As I recall it was almost done at the time. It had potential.

Karen Brooks was another songwriter spending time at the Phoenix X Condominium penthouse. Karen won a Grammy for her work on the 1985 Sesame Street Musical: "Follow That Bird." She had a mini-recording studio replete with a laptop computer full of music set up on the condo's massive dining room table. I was amazed at how sophisticated she was in her technical songwriting approach.

Karen is a lovely person and is easy to talk to. She and I shared creative thoughts and I enjoyed meeting her, as I had never before met a Grammy winner.

I had never really hung out with songwriters before. Sadly for me, I never knew any. As criminal as it sounds, as a product of mainly Louisiana public schools I had never been exposed to music. Growing up I had never read a lick of music or even tried to play an instrument. In retrospect, I still feel cheated in that regard.

Watching the songwriters work I saw how much smaller their playing field is. I noticed how much more demanding writing songs seemed. Stuffing words set to music into such a tiny space was a conundrum that required countless repetitions of trial and error. Over and over they tried different words and phrases, looking for the most meaningful, congruous fit. Without any knowledge of music, it was all such a departure for me. But I liked what I saw. The creative process is always so interesting. Through determined effort something can always come from nothing.

It turned out to everyone's surprise that the young redhead with Johnny was actually forty years old. She was actually older than Johnny, yet looked half his age. Mike chided Johnny, "What is she doing so right that you ain't?"

Johnny just shrugged and laughed, completely used to the fatherly drill.

I looked his way and gave a thumbs up and a smile.

***

On one of those first few cold winter nights in February 2010, Joe and I finally had a chance to sit down and talk about what I was trying to do. Further, we got to know each other better, talking about each other's past and our life experiences. I began to relax more around him.

Joe was impressed when I told him that my mentor is Coach Dale Brown, the former LSU Basketball Coach and international motivational speaker. It was Dale Duward Brown who discovered a twelve-year-old Shaquille O'Neal in Germany, on the Army base where his father was stationed. Joe had heard much of Coach Brown and he told me that he always liked what he stood for, what he represented.

Dale Brown is a tremendous human being. He is the consummate motivator and a man as passionate as he is caring; as his depth of heart is unparalleled. Much of who I am I owe to his loving enthusiasm and interest in my life. I am honored to know, follow and love him.

"Dale Brown is your base mentor?" Joe asked.

"Yes" I told him. "We talked today. He sent me notes to a new book he read. He is a voracious reader, and he takes notes on all the books he reads. He always sends me the notes, which are like Cliff's Notes."

"You are lucky. Not many people can say that."

"Thank you. I think so," I replied. I was flattered; but Joe was setting me up.

"You know Chris…" Joe said before pausing. "It's impressive, all that you have done writing books, but, you know, you could be a lot more useless in life."

It didn't register with me at first. It sounded oxymoronic. I didn't quite get it.

"What does that mean?" I asked.

Joe smiled and repeated.

"It means you could become a lot more useless in life. It is what it is. Don't take things so seriously. Have some fun. Live a little."

I felt guilty. I was pretty sure I knew where he was going, but I didn't want to go there.

"Do you have any fun anymore?" he asked.

"Sure I do," I defended myself.

"Just remember," he said, "Chris, I'm telling you—you can become a lot more useless in life."

I figured that I had a ways to go until I could embrace life or even see it the way Joe did—and for that—I was intensely jealous of Joe Gilchrist. I was jealous—albeit only briefly, over the way he had lived like a teenager for so many years, and more specifically, of the non-conventional tack he'd taken toward living his life in the pursuit of happiness—of all the fun he'd had doing it *his* way. Moreover, Joe had confidently bucked the establishment and created something unique and wildly monetarily successful. That in itself is certainly enviable. In this way, Joe Gilchrist is so different from other Americans, who seem bent on working themselves to death.

Joe finished with his favorite line, "Life is meant to be enjoyed, Chris. The sad thing is that most people never realize it until it's too late."

Joe repeated this turnkey phrase often those first few weeks I knew him, solidifying it as his unofficial mantra, and further impressing upon me his steadfast belief that we have only scratched the surface of this notion we call "having fun." Like anything else, I figured, it seemed we just needed to focus on it more. We needed to plan for it; once we fully knew what it was.

A few days later Joe told me to report rested to the Silver Moon Package Store for a trip to Mobile in the old faded blue Flora-Bama Bus. You may have spotted the Bama Bus before. It is often parked in front of the Silver Moon Package Store, its trademark Flora-Bama logo emblazoned in large print on the side. The excursion, Joe said, was planned to happen with a zany group he half-heartedly called "a bunch of local characters and musicians."

One of the things I quickly realized about Joe is that he loves bringing people together for whatever the reason, that he loves involving various characters, as he always puts it, to "see what happens." It is exactly the premise of the Flora-Bama—to bring all sorts of folks from all walks of life together; and sometimes, magical things can and do happen—like having more fun than you ever expected; which in time, I noticed around Joe Gilchrist, happens more often than not. Frequently you will hear Joe remark, "This is the best life I ever lived!"

The purpose of the trip was to oblige an entrepreneur who had recently built a recording studio, Mud Brick Media Studios, in Mobile. A wealthy gentleman with a penchant for musicians and music, much like Joe, erected the studio and had extended a permanent invitation to all Flora-Bama musicians and performers to use it to record music or high-definition music videos—*free of charge*. Rhonda Hart was one of the musicians who took advantage of the generous offer.

The event held that night was to showcase the new studio and its many production capabilities. Further, there was live musical entertainment and a dinner planned for all of us who attended. Joe told me he wanted us to go to the event because he greatly appreciated the owner's generosity toward trying to help his creative class of singers, songwriters and musicians. He felt it was the least he could do to extend the courtesy and attend the planned event.

As instructed, I arrived at the Silver Moon and boarded the old beat up, faded blue Flora-Bama Bus that looked over twenty years old. It was a slightly smaller version of a standard yellow school bus, but it was not a short bus. It was medium-sized. The rowed seats in the bus had been removed, and in their place were only long benches running along each side. I found a spot early, along with Rhonda Hart and her daughter, Chandra Rose, who also brought a friend. Elaine Petty showed, as did Jason Justice, another regular Flora-Bama performer, along with Sandy and Joe, Bo Roberts, Chris Newbury, and a host of what Joe facetiously called, "victims." These were regulars at the Silver Moon and the Bama—folks that could easily accurately claim that they paid the utilities at the Silver Moon by the amount of leisure time and disposable income spent there.

Joe stashed a couple of coolers of iced adult beverages in the back of the bus, and we enjoyed several on the ride down to Mobile, which took nearly three hours. Normally, if we had not been in a bus full of inebriated individuals who needed to repeatedly stop to urinate, and had we not been in a bus with a maximum speed of fifty miles per hour, we would have made it to Mobile in a little over an hour. It turned out to be a real trip from hell getting down there. Evening traffic in Mobile was bumper-to-bumper. Of course, we made the most of it. In retrospect, it was a fun ride, as the characters aboard were many.

Eventually, we made it to our destination—the multi-million dollar high-performance recording studio and video production facility owned by wealthy benefactors. We received a grand tour of the impressive facility. It was as state-of-the art as it was spacious.

The live musical entertainment that evening was interesting, to say the least. The act featured a young husband and wife duo from Colorado who traveled to Mobile in their tiny mobile home. The husband, a broad fellow, came across as a huge fan of John Denver, as he had, in his best impersonation, assumed his persona; and "Rocky Mountain High" was actually one of the many songs they sang—badly out of key, I should add. It was difficult to endure.

When the break after the first set finally came, many of us wondered aloud in the restroom if there would be a second. It turned out there was, but thank goodness they served dinner during the second set, making it at least somewhat bearable, for oddly, the many accomplished musicians in the audience.

Needless to say, once the show and dinner was over, we were anxious to get out of there. Once we were all back on the bus with fresh cold drinks in our hands, Jason Justice broke the ice.

"Joe, thanks a lot for bringing us all out here." Jason said.

Joe replied, "You're welcome, I just wanted to try and attend because they are trying to help members of our songwriting community…"

Jason Justice quickly interjected, "Yeah, that's great, but you didn't tell us you were taking us to see John Denver's deranged cousin!"

Needless to say, that comment drew a roar of laughter from everyone in the Bama Bus; and the party was on. Things really cut loose after that.

Jason Justice, a Navy veteran, who regularly holds well-attended Sunday morning religious services called "Worship on the Water" at the Flora-Bama outside under the side tent, grabbed a guitar and started wildly playing and singing. Jason is one of those musicians who noticeably puts his heart into everything he plays, and in this instance, he was the catalyst to another fun time. He and Rhonda and Elaine really treated us the entire way back to the bustling Flora-Bama, singing tons of songs and telling countless, hilarious jokes.

Once we returned to a packed Flora-Bama, we told everyone of our wild road trip. It was a really fun time, as I cannot remember laughing as hard as I did on that wacky, early road trip in the Bama Bus to Mobile. The episode made the keen impression on me that Joe Gilchrist really knew how to have fun.

Chapter Two

"Getting to Know Joe"

"He lacked only a few vices to be perfect."

-Marquise de Sevigne

As the Imperial Japanese Army's Kawamura Detachment landed in Iloilo City, Philippines on April 17, 1942, broadening its belligerent grip on the Pacific Rim, Joseph R. Gilchrist was born a war-time baby, the third of three brothers, in Birmingham, Alabama.

When he was a young boy, Joe's family moved south to the Gulf Breeze, Florida area. Joe attended Pensacola High School, following in the footsteps of his two older brothers, David and Lane. Lane, who died in 2009, was a former mayor of Gulf Breeze, Florida (near Pensacola) for over three decades.

After high school graduation, Joe attended Auburn University. Like most, once Joe moved away from home for college, he began to spread his wings. What he did early on during his campus days on the Auburn plains was a most certain foreshadowing of his innate acumen and eventual business career as a successful entrepreneur.

As a sophomore at Auburn, the Flora-Bama's eventual patriarch lived in the Sigma Alpha Epsilon Fraternity house, as his older brother, David, was an SAE. Joe said that tuition in those days was about $90 per semester, a considerable sum, even though today it is about $4,500 for a resident student. Money was tight for Joe, like it was and usually is for all college students. However, he found a quick, sure and easy way to make spending money—by selling cold beer out of his dormitory fridge in the fraternity house. Joe said he operated on an honor system for a while, but that the privilege was quickly abused by the thirsty young upperclassmen. He said he soon had to regrettably keep a lock on his door and strictly monitor beer sales, no doubt a hard-learned lesson for the budding sud salesman.

Joe bought canned beer by the case from a willing local distributor and re-sold it by single cans or six-packs to his fraternity brothers at a handsome profit of about $50 per week, which was what he called, "great drinking money at the time." Joe said even he was surprised when he approached the distributor on the outskirts of Auburn about buying cases of beer for resale at a wholesale, rather than a retail price—and he said yes.

"He likely knew I was re-selling the beer, but he obviously didn't care that I didn't have a license," recalled Joe.

Joe said that at Auburn he was hardly a Rhodes Scholar. "It took me 17 quarters to graduate from Auburn. It should have taken 12. My dad wasn't too happy with me as a result, but I had a lot of fun in college."

Joe said one quarter he spent an inordinate amount of time playing cards. That term he won a smart-looking $5 bridge trophy in exchange for barely passing enough hours to stay academically solvent. However, the borderline B and C student did what all average students who stay in school and pass all required coursework eventually do—he graduated.

After college, Joe initially taught. In 1965, he spent a year teaching chemistry at Pensacola High School—at his old school and in his old classroom. The next year he taught general science in Columbus, Georgia. His last three years of teaching were spent instructing seniors in civics and economics at Pacifica High School in the Orange County, California area.

It has been said that all good business leaders must be good teachers—that they must have the ability to package and transfer knowledge, so this experience undoubtedly had a positive effect on Joe. He explained his decision to abruptly leave the Deep South for the West Coast.

"I was young and single and enjoying life, and California in the 1960's was a great place to be doing that. It seemed that all the characters of America piled up out there."

Joe spent three years sowing wild oats living the California good life. During this time he taught in California, two good friends he met in Pensacola during their flight training visited him. One of these was Al Coley, a former football player from Georgia. Another was Ron Zappardino, a cocky Philadelphia-raised Italian. Joe was destined in life to continue to meet each of these men individually. They remain friends today.

Both of Joe's brothers, Lane and David, proudly served as Navy officers. Because of this Joe developed a deep and lifelong appreciation for people who serve our country in the military.

Joe returned to Pensacola, where he re-acquainted with an old friend who had recently purchased the Townhouse, a motel and lounge on the corner of Palafox and Cervantes streets in the downtown area. The old friend, Charles Liberis, a Pensacola attorney, who still practices there today, hired Joe to run the food and beverage aspect of the business.

"I ran that business from 1970 to 1972 and I learned a lot about how to run a restaurant and bar. I also decided that I no longer wanted to run a place that someone else owned."

***

We have to go back a little further in time to understand how the Flora-Bama came to be. Joe Gilchrist knew Mr. Ted Tampary and his family, who like Joe, were from the Pensacola area. In 1960, or about that time, Connie and Tony Tampary, Ted's sons, drove Joe through the State of Alabama toward the State of Florida to a point which is today Orange Beach, Alabama. As they stood overlooking the Alabama Point inlet, to the east into the State of Florida, Connie motioned toward a span of beach that disappeared into the horizon. Connie explained to Joe that his family owned several miles of that beach, nearly as far as they could see. Joe was reportedly unimpressed, because there was no access to the land—and more importantly, there was no road.

From that day forward the Tampary family lobbied hard and tried to convince the states of Alabama and Florida to each build half of a bridge that would connect the area transected by Perdido Pass. The State of Florida refused, and instead ceded the project, and their state line, which was formerly at the Pass, giving up about a mile or so of prime beach real estate to the State of Alabama, which at the time, had only 37 miles of coastline. The State of Alabama thereafter built the bridge over Perdido Pass and the road all the way to Florida entirely on its own (completed in 1962), and in return got the new and improved state line we know today, right where the Flora-Bama now rests. It should also be noted that the State of Alabama received Ono Island in this agreement. The State of Florida, in turn, built a road from the Pensacola area up to the new state line, where the Flora-Bama was originally built, shortly thereafter.

After the two state roads were finally connected, the first bar to spring up on Perdido Key was an ancient, broken-down river boat known as The River Queen, owned by local Escambia County politicians. It was reportedly a bona fide honky-tonk, replete with an unassuming red clay parking lot. Larry Strickland said the place was full of "Drinking, gambling, prostitution and drug smuggling…a virtual frontier land back in those days." Joe corroborated this statement, explaining that the place was much like an unincorporated territory back then. Joe said that it was a really wild place, with a cast of characters engaged in a plethora of illegal activities. When the place was finally shuttered one of the participants was so large that when taken to the Escambia County Jail there was no cell large enough to contain him, so they improvised and chained him to a tree until the Feds picked him up.

As mentioned, the Tampary family began building the original Flora-Bama two years after the state line was moved. On the day before it opened, in 1964, however, it was burned to the ground. The rumor at the time of the razing was that the overzealous owners of the River Queen lit the place ablaze because they wanted to end the new competition for the area's budding alcohol sales. The resourceful Tampary's, undaunted, immediately began to rebuild the place. It was re-opened a few months later, as soon as possible, in 1964.

One must understand that in 1964, the Flora-Bama was virtually in the middle of nowhere. In those days, virgin beach property existed on all sides of The Line. Further, the area still maintained its natural, untouched look and feel. Joe told me he remembers thirty foot sand dunes. There was no modern condominium development. There was only the tiny Flora-Bama, as it had not grown into the destination it is today, and a few mom and pop beach houses. To give you an even better perspective, the place was so far out in the boonies that when it rained the telephones would fail to work for up to two days at a time because of cheap wiring consisting of a single, brittle strand connecting everyone to the main lines. Further, there was little police protection, which really made it interesting.

Because of the fire and its rumored starters—the ruffians who ran the River Queen, a large, intimidating night watchman, Mr. Frank Brown, a muscular black man and former prize fighter, was hired to protect the rebuilt Flora-Bama Lounge and Package Store. A dual pistol-toting Mr. Frank worked there from midnight to 8:00 a.m., six days of the week, watching over the place until the morning came and a new day at the Flora-Bama could begin without instance. The Tamparys were intent on protecting their investment.

In the early days of the Flora-Bama, the package store was practically the only thing going in the area. However, as traffic began to increase along the new highway, local populations and businesses grew, and the Flora-Bama Lounge legend spread accordingly, to match a growing, thirsty demand.

The Flora-Bama forthwith became a beacon for Alabama residents seeking a reprieve from Baldwin County's restrictive blue laws precluding Sunday alcohol sales. When the Tampary family added a tiny bar behind the store in 1964, it was a predictable, immediate hit, creating a loyal, local clientele of patronizing Flora-Bama fans.

***

In April 1978, Joe purchased the original, ramshackle watering hole, The Flora-Bama Lounge and Package Store, owned by the Tampary family. It wasn't easy, but Joe, through determination and perseverance, finally acquired and imbued his unmistakable brand upon the place that would grow to be called the beloved "Pumphouse on the Line."

The name Flora-Bama is logical in its design, because the bar actually rests mostly in Florida.   Nevertheless, ironically, most everyone who works and regularly plays there affectionately calls it "The Bama." As an aside, the Flora-Bama Old S.A.L.T.S. Marina and parking lot on the north side across the street from the iconic bar, however, is located on Old River in the State of Alabama. Sometimes you will see its entire, original title in print: *Flora-Bama Lounge, Package, Oyster Bar & Grill."*

Author Tom Dorsey aptly observed that the Flora-Bama "looked as if it was built by the enemies of the owners." While it's a crafted line certainly deserving of a laugh, I cannot speak to its veracity, as I don't know Joe or Pat to have enemies. Although, I do believe many are jealous of them and their successes. Nevertheless, the point is well-taken. The structure itself is a makeshift hodgepodge of building materials—but loveable just the same by anyone who has been there.

Joe explained that acquiring the Flora-Bama was no easy feat.

"I kept trying to work out a deal with him, but I had to get approval to buy the liquor license before he (Mr. Tampary) would agree to lease the bar to me."

With the help of a friend he made at Auburn, a Pensacola lobbyist, Joe was able to get approval on the liquor license. As a result, he took over the Flora-

Bama on April 17, 1978, which happened to be his 36th birthday. In the beginning, Joe worked tirelessly to fulfill his vision for the Flora-Bama. Twelve to sixteen hour days were common.

"I worked all the time, seven days a week during the first year. I remember taking one day off during that time to go fishing. I was so tired, that I fell asleep on the boat."

Success came from the hard work at the Flora-Bama, and after nearly a decade of flying solo, Joe partnered with Pat McClellan in 1986. A former Public Relations officer for the United States Navy, Pat understood people and promotions. Further, Pat's operational prowess complemented well Joe's efforts at a time when the Flora-Bama was really just starting to become what it is today—an international beach destination.

McClellan came to the Perdido Key area in the early 1980's to join the Navy's flight program. Like so many, he immediately fell in love with the place and never left. A graduate of the University of Minnesota, Pat comes across more like an Alabama or Auburn alum, as he is as friendly and accommodating as his muscular frame is sturdy and powerful. He is also, like Joe, an astute business person and an equally natural promoter.

Pat further explained his role at the iconic watering hole, "The Flora-Bama is the place where you can go to be yourself and nobody cares…A good saloonkeeper doesn't talk about politics, religion or sex, and we never root for Alabama, Auburn, Florida or Florida State…we instead just ask for the best team to win. And we never, ever root for Notre Dame. As a proprietor, I look for overtime and extra innings…The main thing is we're here for people's enjoyment and relaxation and to take some of the cares of the world out of their minds, maybe; and to get them to enjoy life for a while."

Joe and Pat work well together, as they both enjoy having fun. In 1998, they teamed up with Ono Island architect Brad Patterson, Connie Tampary and the ostensible developer Dusty Rhodes to announce a huge real estate sale and development.

Brad Patterson said that in late March he got a call from Joe asking for a favor.

"I need you to do something for me," Joe asked.

"Sure," said Brad, who like so many of the regulars, is a most fun and interesting character. He is always laughing and having a good time.

Joe asked Brad to draw up a rough set of architectural plans. Joe and Pat had finally caved to development pressures—they were planning to build a massive vacation condo development straddling the two state lines where the Flora-Bama was.

The venture was tabbed, "The Wayward Home for Lost Musicians." On paper it consisted of two massive towers—the Flora and the Bama, with a connecting "Elvis Presley Sky Bridge" formed in the shape of a guitar. Brad's sketches even included an elaborate, transparent bubble over the Flora-Bama, inspiring an overall look reminiscent of the Monte Carlo Casino in Monaco.

Joe and Pat sent out press releases regarding the massive new real estate development in the days leading to April first. Predictably, all three local television stations and several print outlets showed to verify that the Flora-Bama owners had indeed sold out to real estate interests, and that the iconic beach bar would never be the same.

After unveiling Brad's CAD-aided renderings of the development to the unsuspecting, salivating media representatives, Joe and Pat ended the presentation with an impromptu declaration of "April Fools!" According to Brad, the reporters who showed for the event were not happy with the joke—even though Joe and Pat provided pizza and champagne for their consumption. However, some media outlets reported the stunt, which amounted to valuable free publicity.

As usual, at the Flora-Bama, things are not always what they appear or are planned to be. It turned out that Dusty Rhodes was on the lamb for writing fake bank checks for his $300,000 motor home, his $100,000 speed boat and was apparently only temporarily out of jail, as he was soon returned to public custody shortly thereafter. Everybody liked Dusty and we were sad to see him go. Happy April Fool's!

Pat shares Joe's passion for community involvement. He and his lovely wife Sheryl, and their family are active philanthropists, like Joe, as they enjoy giving back to the community that has given them so much.

***

Joe's vision for the Flora-Bama has not wavered since he began in 1978. The underlying theme has always been about the music, and in that same vein, the songwriter and the musician. Joe's deep abiding love and devout appreciation for live music, musicians and songwriters, and the joy they bring to the world, inspired him to create a special place where artists could celebrate their craft by creating and showcasing their music and songs. More importantly, he wanted to create a place where people from all walks of life can come and enjoy what he and many others refer to as some of the best music anywhere in the country, rock, kick-butt country, folk, jazz, bluegrass and blues. Further, he wanted to encourage what he calls, a "rare, cross-cultural experience where people meet others that are distinctly different than them."

By making live performances the centerpiece of the Flora-Bama—there is scheduled live music there seven days a week—Joe has effectively re-introduced to the world the addictive charm of watching musicians perform in real time. Today most people get their music through the radio, digital downloads, and more often now through the Internet (Pandora or iHeartRadio) or compact discs. Although there are and always will be large, national concert tours, small, intimate venues offer a unique, nearly-forgotten opportunity for music lovers everywhere.

The Flora-Bama is a place where visitors can not only enjoy the original work of each artist—it is also a place where they can get to know the artist, as it is where they regularly play their music. Local members—who religiously purchase membership cards on the first of every year, know this well. Because of this, I like to refer to the Flora-Bama as a particularly funky brand of "Disneyland for Adults," with the characters—the main attractions—being the musicians, their performances and sometimes even the patrons, of course; as it is easily one of the best people-watching places on the planet. Further, you can request songs at the Flora-Bama. Recently a clothesline on a pulley has been slung from the main stage all the way up to the second floor balcony. Patrons now use it and a clothespin to run request notes and sometimes cash to the musicians on stage.

Joe has reminded untold numbers visiting the Flora-Bama that there are accomplished artists everywhere who are as talented as the named stars who play daily on the radio. It's just that they haven't gotten the big break they need. Although, some artists have gotten that break playing at the Flora-Bama, because it introduces them to a vast network of talented musicians and songwriters, as well as the managers and fans who help support them.

Until meeting Joe and training my eye on him and his fabled operation, I never fully realized that the Flora-Bama has live music daily—that you can go there every day of the week and enjoy live music. Because of this oversight I did not understand that it was, by the originator's design, the main draw of the place, and the backdrop against which everything else there transpired.

Joe Gilchrist has aptly been called by Karen Brooks, the Grammy-winning songwriter I mentioned, "a muse." It is actually an excellent metaphor to describe him. Consider its formal definition:

Muse (myo͞oz)

n.

1. Greek Mythology Any of the nine daughters of Mnemosyne and Zeus, each of whom presided over a different art or science.

2. muse

a. A guiding spirit.

b. A source of inspiration.

3. muse A poet.

Originally one of the nine daughters of Mnemosyne and Zeus, each of them (muses) presided over a different area of the arts or science. As a muse, Joe's area of the arts is undoubtedly music, and the musicians, and the often-forgotten songwriters who make the whole world sing.

Joe also understands well that when the music industry was hit by the download craze, it adversely affected the songwriters, who make only a fraction of what the artists make for each cut. When the artists began losing sales revenues to the download phenomenon, the songwriters also lost proportionately, making their small sliver of pie all the much thinner. Recognizing their plight, Joe has fully embraced the difficult task of helping all of them—the humble songwriters and musicians who make us all sing. And for that alone he will be well-remembered.

***

On the first Friday of every month Joe gets together with good friends at a popular restaurant and pub, McGuire's, in nearby Pensacola, Florida, about thirty miles from the Flora-Bama. Like the Flora-Bama, McGuire's is a local institution. The owner of the establishment—which has over an estimated half million dollars in American singles, fives and ten dollar bills stapled to its ceiling and walls—Bill McGuire Martin, is the hosting member of Flat Earth Society, which includes several other prominent businessmen, lawyers, judges, doctors and authors, like W.E.B. Griffin, of nearby Fairhope, Alabama, where I have a home, and General William L. "Spider" Nyland of the United States

Marine Corps, a former Assistant Commandant (2002-2005), among other notable characters.

McGuire's is somewhat of an anomaly in the Deep South. A true Irish pub and eatery, it is a massive place, with an unmistakable, quintessential Irish flair. The men of Flat Earth meet in a remotely obscure corner of the novelty restaurant, far away from the beaten crowd, around a circular table with a smaller spinning food top. Usually there are about eight to ten different gentlemen in attendance, all similarly well-intentioned—to seriously lament, praise and pontificate everything and anything worthy of idle discourse; even many a bad joke is told, but it does get interesting, particularly when the bill reaches one hundred dollars.

The gentlemen in the Flat Earth Society maintain an Epicurean tilt at their monthly gatherings. Wine, whiskey, beer, ribs, nachos, loaded chunky bleu cheese and chips, chicken, steak, pork sausage, and chocolate cake along with vanilla and chocolate-covered ice cream for dessert are the usual; and it quickly adds up to real money. When the bill tops one hundred dollars the waitress ritually brings the ticket to the table. Everyone seated around the circle that has not yet had to pay a hundred-dollar ticket, must flip a quarter. Someone calls the quarter. The winner(s) is/are out, and the process is repeated until a loser is declared (last person flipping) to pay for the round. Once the bill is paid, that payer is then exempt from having to pay again, making for what is always a fun sidebar to an extremely light-hearted and enjoyable feast.

Regarding food, I would be remiss without mentioning the fact that Joe is an excellent cook. On many occasions Joe has thrown together a meal for us on short notice. It's always hearty and tasty. Further, he never wastes food, or anything else, for that matter. He is always prudent with leftovers, saving chicken and beef bones that others would be inclined to throw away in order to make soups and other delectable creations. He is a lover of animals, always going out of his way to provide for forlorn felines and canines; and he seems to always acquire new ones.

On one occasion that Joe cooked for me at his house on Old River, I realized that in many ways he remains the youthful, 18-year old Auburn freshman who sold beer to his frat brothers. Joe made us what I would cautiously typify as "chicken stew." It was a soup made of leftovers from the previous night's supper.

We sat down to watch the popular *Band of Brothers* series that Joe had on DVD. Joe is a huge fan of military history and lore, and he loves to watch anything historically significant on the topic. I sat in a recliner and Joe sat on his couch before a coffee table loaded with drinking cups, magazines, business and personal mail and a host of other worldly items. It barely had room for his bowl.

Joe placed his brimming stew bowl on the coffee table before him. He took a regular, square, thin paper napkin, unfolded it and tucked it neatly in the front of his shirt collar, creating a bib. What he did next completely surprised me, as I had never seen such a thing.

With both hands Joe carefully lifted the coffee table, bringing it up to within inches of his face—and it stayed—as it was connected to the legs by telescoping metal arms which acted like an accordion. Once he had the table positioned where he wanted it to be, it remained. It was a funny moment, as Joe looked like an aging Inspector Gadget eating a meal. I could only laugh.

Joe also introduced me to a most refreshing non-alcoholic, summer drink. He showed me that if you take *Fresca* Original Citrus soda and mix it with black cherry or pomegranate juice, that you have a wonderfully tasty and bubbly, thirst-quenching beverage. I recommend it. It's great when you are at the beach and are looking for a refreshing non-alcoholic alternative.

Although Joe has not had a nine-to-five job in many years, he nevertheless works hard. He is seemingly always on his cell phone trying to promote various events at the Flora-Bama and for his many business-owning friends in the community. Of course, he plays equally hard. He has fun. However, as long as I have known Joe and have ran with him, I have never known him to abuse alcohol. Joe is a social drinker, but outside of an occasional *Coors Light* beer, I have not seen him drink to excess.

It seems that Joe enjoys much more than anything the socializing aspects and prospects of the Flora-Bama and the Silver Moon—of being able to recognize and fully dignify the many faithful characters and old friends who religiously frequent his business place. Of course, he equally enjoys meeting new characters and making new friends. In this way, Joe is keenly aware of his proprietary role; and I would go as far to say that it is one of the main reasons why the Flora-Bama has been so successful through the years—because of Joe's acute attention to customer service. Much like the fabled *Cheers* bar in Boston, Massachusetts that was made into a hugely popular *NBC* television series, Joe has created a seemingly unquenchable watering hole with the same endearing tagline, "Where everybody knows your name."

Longtime Flora-Bama employee Robin Lusk, who began working there thirty years ago when she was only 16, said that through the years she can recall that the bar's best times were when the bands playing and the bartenders were all on the same page—and when Joe was at his best slowly working the Flora-Bama crowd, letting each and every one of them know he truly appreciated their patronage. "Whenever you had the bartenders in sync with the band and Joe was out there shaking hands, things were always at their best," she said.

A natural networker and devout philanthropist, Joe is a founding member of the Alabama Gulf Coast Chamber of Commerce and the Perdido Key, Florida Chamber of Commerce. Joe's greatest wish is that the people who have come to the area in recent years would not only contribute their fair share to the area, but would also respectfully not forget the combination of characters who have been and will remain the real founders of the magical place to which he's devoted the last 33 years.

Joe married once and divorced. That union produced a daughter, Marjorie Gilchrist Kussin. Marjorie married Greg Kussin, and gave Joe two grand-daughters, Hannah and Olivia, whom he loves spending time with whenever his busy schedule and theirs permit.

Chapter Three

Ivan the Terrible

"It ain't a fit night out for man or beast."

-*W.C. Fields, excerpted from "The Fatal Glass of Beer," 1933*

Prior to Hurricane Ivan, the Flora-Bama was a makeshift compound of loosely assembled party areas. It consisted of the indoor and outdoor decks, tents, walkways, the older package store, a multi-level interior bar, stages, a pool room and precious, indoor bathrooms. That, however, was *before* Ivan the Terrible struck unmercifully on Northwest, Florida.

On September 16, 2004, Hurricane Ivan scored a direct hit on the Flora-Bama, causing catastrophic damage throughout the extended Orange Beach, Perdido Key and Pleasure Island areas. The main building at the Flora-Bama's peculiar entrance was destroyed, and most of the bar's other sections were either decimated or heavily damaged. The place was wrecked.

After the storm, the Flora-Bama was partially closed for business for nearly a year while rebuilding efforts commenced. The original top deck survived the storm in fairly good condition; and the stair bar area below the top deck, though full of sand, remained virtually intact. The stairs leading from the deck bar to the top deck survived, but the main stage area near the deck bar lost its roof. This area was replaced with a tent-like canopy until major renovations commenced in the spring of 2011.

The loss of the main building that held the conspicuous, tortuous main entranceway, was particularly regrettable, as it had served the establishment well, always making somewhat of a fun mystery the anticipation of entering the Flora-Bama.

Despite the extensive damage done by Ivan, many of the old regulars, undoubtedly longing for their favorite haunt, said that it "looked just fine." Joe reportedly quipped, "Even when the church is destroyed they still hold service."

A useful boardwalk allowing beach access was constructed after the storm. Also, an outdoor stage beneath a large tent was erected to complement the indoor main stage that survived the violent storm surge. As a result of the loss of usable square footage, much of the post-Ivan operating property was covered by trailers of some sort or another. In fact, at the time of this writing, the main office was housed in a trailer. Some of the women's port-o-let facilities were also housed in a trailer. A trailer serving barbecue and other food is usually active during peak times, and numerous trailers on the property are used for storage of major supplies, making the place look at times—like a makeshift trailer park. It is not surprising, however, as many of the Flora-Bama's adoring patrons live in trailers; sort of like I did during my times on the island. And in hindsight, there certainly isn't anything wrong with that!

I am certain there are working stiffs somewhere who would gladly trade their mundane nine to five existence to live in an air-conditioned trailer next to the sparkling Gulf of Mexico and the lively Flora-Bama. It is a fantastic place to do nothing except meet interesting people and have fun.

Despite being closed for many months while repairing and rebuilding during Ivan's aftermath, the Flora-Bama's parched and laugh-starved crowd swarmed right back to the endearing beach bar as soon as it reopened its waterlogged doors. During the rebuild the Silver Moon across the street from the Flora-Bama became a temporary replacement.

**

Ivan was devastating. Just before it made landfall on the United States mainland, the hurricane's eye wall weakened and its southwestern quadrant nearly disappeared. Around 2 a.m. Central Daylight Time September 16, 2004, the storm made landfall in Gulf Shores, Alabama as a Category 3 hurricane with 120 miles per hour winds. Some hurricane information agencies clocked Ivan's winds near 130 miles per hour upon landfall in Alabama and northwestern Florida. Ivan continued inland, maintaining hurricane strength until it was over central Alabama.

The storm weakened rapidly over land and became a tropical depression while it was still over the State of Alabama. Ivan lost tropical storm characteristics on September 18, 2004, while crossing the State of Virginia. Later that day, the remnants of Ivan drifted off the U.S. mid-Atlantic coast into the Atlantic Ocean, while the low pressure disturbance continued to dump rain on the eastern Atlantic Seaboard of the United States.

Further demonstrating the storm's strength was the fact that the city of Demopolis, Alabama, over 100 miles inland in west-central Alabama, endured wind gusts estimated at 90 miles per hour while Montgomery saw wind gusts in the 60 miles per hour to 70 miles per hour range at the height of the storm.

The heaviest damage as Ivan made landfall on the U.S. coastline was observed in Baldwin County, Alabama, where the storm's eye and concentric eye wall made landfall. High surf and wind brought extensive damage to Orange Beach, particularly near the border with Florida, where the Flora Bama lies. There, multi-story condominium buildings reinforced with concrete were undermined to the point of collapse by Ivan's storm surge of 14 feet. In addition to the extensive damage to Lower Alabama, there was harm done to the state's electrical grid. At the height of the roaming power outages, Alabama Power reported 489,000 subscribers had lost electrical power—roughly half of its statewide subscriber base.

Hurricane Ivan killed 64 people in the Caribbean—mainly in Grenada and Jamaica—three in Venezuela, and 25 in the United States, including 14 in Florida. Thirty-two more deaths in the United States were indirectly attributed to Hurricane Ivan, making it a particularly deadly storm. Tornadoes spawned by the hurricane struck communities along concentric arcs on the leading edge of the storm. In Florida, Blountstown, Marianna, and Panama City Beach suffered three devastating tornadoes. Ivan caused over $13 billion in damages in the United States and $3 billion in U.S. Dollars in the Caribbean.

Ivan was a terrible reminder that life on the coast can be perilous. However, it was also a reminder of how resilient the people who live on the island are. As destructive as the storm was, the community was equally effective at rebuilding.

During Ivan, Joe retreated in a motor home to Tunica, Mississippi. While there gambling at one of the Indian casinos Joe saw on television that the storm was making landfall apparently right over the Flora-Bama. He said, "That's when I knew how severely challenged my near future was going to be."

In Alan Brockman's documentary on the Flora-Bama, "The Last Great American Roadhouse," there is extensive video footage of the Flora-Bama just after Ivan hit. In one of the surreal scenes depicting total devastation, Joe surveys first-hand the full destruction of the Flora-Bama's main bar, which is inundated by several tons of sugar white sand. Louisiana-born Singer/songwriter Johnny Barbados brings an incredulous Joe an unopened bottle of whiskey that somehow survived the destructive onslaught, and then sings Joe a song he quickly wrote about the destructive storm and how they will ultimately rebuild. It was as poignant as it ultimately proved foretelling.

Today, seven years later, there are few visual reminders of one of the worst storms to ever hit Paradise Island.

Chapter Four

Pleasure Island

"Florida isn't so much a place where one goes to reinvent oneself, as it is a place where one goes if one no longer wished to be found."

-Doug Coupland

The Flora-Bama Lounge & Package Store lies in a sub-tropical island area possessing a rich and storied past. Some might even call it a romantic, pirate-laden history.

The Flora-Bama is just inside the State of Florida, with only a small western portion resting in Alabama. It hugs a narrow, island strip of white sparkling sand from Perdido Pass to the Intracoastal Canal, running perpendicular to the tide, separating Ono Island and Old River from the Gulf of Mexico. This coastal area nestled against a gleaming blue-green backdrop is one that has seen much human activity over the past few hundred years of its recorded history.

According to the book *The Best Place to Be: The History of Orange Beach*, by lifelong resident Margaret Childress Long, published in 2007, the Orange Beach/Perdido Key area now home to the Flora-Bama was once amidst a vast network of primitive indigenous Indian fishing villages, evidenced by discovered remnants of human-built temples and mounds. These early Indian settlements included the handicraft of the Appalachee of Northwest Florida, the Chickasaw, Cherokee, Choctaw and the Creek. These indigenous tribes did not live permanently in the area, but instead—much like their modern human counterparts—lived there seasonally during the teeming, temperate months, taking advantage of the area's natural abundance of fish, game and wildlife.

There were many early European explorers to the dual state region. Records indicate that they may have landed in the Orange Beach area in the late Fifteenth Century, when Columbus was making his more famous journey. In 1497, Amerigo Vespucci made several voyages to the gulf coast area from

Spain. Some contend that Vespucci, in doing so, even mapped the entire Mobile Bay area. During this same period, noted Juan Ponce de Leon, the purported seeker of the ever-elusive Fountain of Youth, explored and charted the Florida Territory.

In 1539, Spanish Explorer Hernando DeSoto charted the vast, uncharted Southeastern gulf area. In 1682, the noted Rene' Robert Cavalier Sieur De LaSalle, traveled the entire Mississippi River from Canada, thereafter claiming all lands affected by the river as French.

During the American Colonial period pirate ships roamed the navigable waterways and trenches of the greater Orange Beach area. Pirate's Cove, just east of Wolf Bay, is named for these early area explorers. Famed pirate and warrior Jean Lafitte of The War of 1812 fame hulled his ships in nearby Perdido Bay east of the Flora-Bama.

Joe told me that one of the first characters he met in the area was Billy Walker, who led an earlier life that would remind one of Jean Lafitte. Joe said Billy's mother was a wonderful character and that she used to say, "I'm gonna have my boy Billy come talk to you." Joe said that Billy, a six-foot three inch rather roguish fellow, came and introduced himself and that they became great friends.

"Billy was always a force to be reckoned with, and I was always glad that he was my friend—and still am."

Legend also has it that pirates of Jean Lafitte's ilk, routing from Pensacola to New Orleans, often found safe harbor between plunders in the shallow, protective confines of Perdido Bay. Some insist that they buried some of this golden booty deep in the native sands, as the area's many coves and inlets would have provided various excellent hideout opportunities for these early adventurers; as well as launching spots for their regular raids on wealthy merchant crafts plying their way along the gulf coast on their journey home to England or Spain.

Directly east of the Flora-Bama is the small community of Perdido Key, Florida, part of the Gulf Islands National Seashore. It is a fragile barrier island consisting of fine quartz sand bound by plants adapted to this harsh saltwater environment. The Key provides habitat for many shore birds, small animals, mullet and nesting sea turtles. The grass beds of the Perdido Key Sound are the nursing grounds of 95 percent of all commercially harvested marine species. Incessant wind and wave actions are the dynamic forces that constantly reshape this postcard picturesque island.

In 2004, Hurricane Ivan damaged many of the manmade structures on Perdido Key. Nevertheless there are remaining recognizable manmade features of the island. Fort McRee was one of them, located on the island's eastern end. This large brick fort was built by the United States Army Corps of Engineers in 1837, along with nearby Forts Barrancas and Pickens, to defend Pensacola Pass and the United States Naval Yard. Fort McRee was damaged during the Civil War and was eventually claimed by wave action and natural erosion.

Perdido Key, Florida is located in Escambia County, Florida, between Pensacola, Florida and Orange Beach, Alabama. The Florida portion of the Gulf Islands National Seashore is located at the island's east end. A narrow strip of sand less than a few hundred yards wide, Perdido Key stretches some 16 miles (26 km) from Perdido Pass Bridge near Orange Beach, Alabama, to just across from Santa Rosa Island near Pensacola, Florida.

To the south of Perdido Key is the Gulf of Mexico with its baby powder white sand beaches and clear emerald waters. North of Perdido Key is Old River and the Intracoastal Waterway. Just north of Old River is privately-owned Ono Island, Alabama. Northeast of Ono and separated by the Intracoastal Waterway (ICW) is a small peninsula called "Innerarity Point" or "Innerarity Island," a private, gated community of mostly single family homes and townhomes. Many say that the funky Innerarity Island area reminds them much of the Florida Keys.

Nearly all of these local waterways are accessible by boat and can give passage to the Gulf of Mexico via the Alabama Pass in Orange Beach or the major harbor entrance of Pensacola Pass. These waterways are: Old River, Intracoastal Waterway (ICW), Perdido Bay, Pensacola Bay, Escambia Bay, Black Water River, Perdido River, Styx River and a maze of navigable canals, bayous and lakes. These inland waterways have historically provided the area protection from violent storms and hurricanes, and are a popular anchor for waterfront homes.

Perdido Key is also home to the endangered, but certainly controversial, Perdido Key Beach Mouse. The small white and gray mouse weighing only a few ounces camouflages well with the white quartz sand of the northern Gulf coast beaches. The rodent feeds primarily on the seeds of sea oats and bluestem, but it will occasionally devour insects.

The Perdido Key beach mouse is controversial because it was listed as an endangered species in 1985. Some blame encroaching housing as a factor.

But, Joe has told me that with 65% of the island existing as federal, state and local park lands, the diminished population is more due to natural causes. However, hurricanes have also taken their toll on the endangered mammal. Nevertheless, the Beach Mouse is a field mouse that is isolated on the key; but it remains a contentious issue.

Like much of its surrounding coastal area, the history and folklore of the Perdido Key area is as fascinating as it is beautiful. As 17th Century Spanish and French explorers navigated the local waterways of Perdido Key, the Spanish held Panzacola (later Pensacola) to the east and the French held Maubila (later Mobile) to the west. As legend has it, a boundary was needed to separate the two new world empires.

Early Spanish and French explorers had rumored of a bay to the west of Pensacola that could serve as a divider between the two European territories. However, although the interests of both Spain and France would seek this elusive bay, it was for a considerable time, a mystery.

In 1693, Don Carlos Siquenza, a noted cartographer, was sent by the Spanish Government to find the entrance to this lost bay. His continued expeditions to find the gap went largely unsuccessful, until one day while surveying by ship what is today the Alabama coastline, a fierce storm descended, forcing Siquenza to reef his sails. A nearby tribal Indian chief who had a rapport with past Spanish explorers, recognized the ship's difficult time and guided it through a theretofore unknown deep water channel into the safe harbor of an awaiting back bay. Siquenza soon realized that he had finally found the elusive, lost entrance and fittingly named it "Perdido Bay." Perdido means "lost" in Spanish.

***

Although a middle-class black community thrived in the Perdido Key area subsequent to the Civil War, it could hardly be found once the overtly racist, Separate But Equal Jim Crow Laws of the late nineteenth and early twentieth century were established. By the 1930's, some sixty-five years after the bitter North-South conflict, one of Northwest Florida's only beaches available to people of color was on Perdido Key. This beach is known as Johnson Beach, named after Rosamond Johnson, Jr., the first black person from Escambia County Florida killed in the Korean War. Joe said that today, part of the great mix of characters in the area includes Alvin Wingate and his family, who are people of color.

Rosamond died a hero in brave service of his country, rescuing fellow soldiers until his life was quickly taken by an enemy bullet. After the conflict, the Escambia County-owned recreation area for blacks was named Johnson Beach in honor of its homegrown hero. The area became part of the Gulf Islands National Seashore on May 8, 1973, and a commemorative bronze plaque bearing his name and likeness was established at Johnson Beach in June 1996. The signifying placard reads:

> "In grateful memory of Private Rosamond Johnson, Jr. RA 14289828, Infantry, who died in service of his country in the military operations in Korea on July 26, 1950. He stands in the unspoken line of patriots who have dared to die that freedom might live, and grow, and increase its blessings. Freedom lives, and through it, he lives – in a way that humbles the undertakings of most men. He crossed the 38th Parallel three times. The first two times, he carried back wounded. The third time, he was killed before he could return. May 18, 1933 – July 26, 1950."

Of course, today, all of the area's beaches are open to all people, regardless of race, color or national origin. Annually the local chamber of commerce and other organizations are proud to sponsor a memorial service for Rosamond Johnson.

Chapter Five
Getting Started

"Music is love in search of a word."
-*Sidney Lanier*

In order to create a unique place where everyone could come and enjoy the wonder of live music, Joe Gilchrist needed musicians—preferably those with singing and songwriting talent.

Joe began his ingenious entertainment odyssey at the Flora-Bama with primarily three male musicians: Ken Lambert, Jimmy Louis and Jay Hawkins. Two of the talented original trio—Louis and Hawkins, can still be found playing the Flora-Bama, some thirty-plus years after its inauspicious beginning. The other, Ken Lambert, has had a change of heart.

Ken Lambert is the kind of guy you can learn from. He's spent a lifetime of embracing hard-learned lessons toward getting to the peaceful place he's found as a pastor who regularly mentors prison inmates. A born-again Christian, Ken has finally embraced his savior, Jesus Christ, replacing the heartache, despair and pain of his former life as a drinking, drugging, honky-tonk musician—with love, hope and promise.

Ken arrived at the Redneck Riviera in the late 1970's via Atlanta, Georgia, where he was an early mainstay at the popular Underground Atlanta entertainment district. He later moved to Pensacola where he found favor among the many patrons of the equally popular Seville Quarters. Ken is a powerful artist. He has an obvious gift with words, but the manner in which he delivers them in song is always worth the price of admission. He is a master of his fabled craft and when you watch him perform it always shines through.

Fueled by consummate Nashville performers, the Flora-Bama has many seasoned entertainers—people who can successfully maintain the attention of the crowd, and please them.

Ken said that soon after he moved to Pensacola and started playing, he met and fell in love with another artist, Susie Storm, who just happened to be the girlfriend of "Broadway" Joe Namath, the flamboyant, former Alabama Crimson Tide and New York Jets quarterback known universally for his great legs, excessive drinking and penchant for the wildly unpredictable.

Ken said that Joe Gilchrist heard him play guitar and sing one night in the old Townhouse in downtown Pensacola, and that afterward Joe asked him to play at his new place down on the Florida and Alabama state line. Like all underpaid musicians, Ken was just happy to get another gig to help pay the bills. He obliged, and later, after Joe acquired the Flora-Bama, Ken became the first hired musical talent at the new Flora-Bama, under the ownership of the young, upstart proprietor, Joe Gilchrist.

Ken said that during the Flora-Bama's early days, drinking and partying and raising hell was a regular part of his show, although in hindsight he is not proud of it. Ken was known to get drunk and downright rowdy during his early performances. During one thoughtless rendition, he reportedly shot a hole in fellow musician Jay Hawkins' hat, which hung on the wall.

Ken, who some say sounds a lot like Willie Nelson, once penned a song titled, "We can Kill 'Em'," referring to all politicians. A borrowed line from the tune goes like this:

"String 'em up and run 'em through…politics may not be the oldest profession, but the results are the same…"

Of course, the audience at the Flora-Bama, which is generally conservative, staunchly pro-American and mostly anti-government, loves this sort of off-the-cuff thing, which always gets Ken, the consummate entertainer, to retort, in kind:

"I'm glad you folks stopped by here and not some trashy place down the road."

Ken nostalgically recalled how it all began at the Line.

"Joe used to have me play at what we called at the time, the "New Flora-Bama." In the beginning, there wasn't much. But, Joe would sell beer and booze to customers in the old little package store out front. After ringing them up he'd ask them if they would like to go in the back and enjoy some live music. He'd offer to put their purchases in the cooler while they did just that. If they accepted his offer, he'd walk them out back and introduce them to me on stage and then they would sit down and listen to the music. They usually came back, and it quickly caught on. Others started coming as well and that's how it all got started. Joe always focused on the crowds, making sure his musicians had a listening audience."

Back in the 1980's Ken Lambert and Joe actually lived together for a while in a house on Inerarity Island. Joe recalled that they had a hot tub in the backyard of this house, which was on a canal leading to nearby Perdido Bay. Joe said that he and Ken were enjoying the hot tub with two lady friends early one morning, before the sunrise, as they had been up all night. Joe said it was just the four of them in the hot tub, wearing only their smiles, as clothing was, "always optional in those days," as he put it.

Joe explained that they were enjoying themselves at that early hour, when all of a sudden, a shrimper and his teenage son, riding through a thin veil of fog in a small shrimp boat, passed by in the canal behind the house, visibly close to where they were in the hot tub. Joe said that the two girls they were with stood, despite their nakedness, and waved and yelled at the passing father and son. The dad, obviously pre-occupied by the naked surprise, paid little attention to steering the vessel, as it rammed the side of the canal, quickly depositing his teenage son into the shallow drink. Joe said they all got a huge laugh out of the incident.

After Ken arrived at the Flora-Bama in 1978, it began a serendipitous chain reaction. It turned out that he had landed in the right place at just the right time. A year later, the unflappable Jay Hawkins arrived; and then the unmistakable Jimmy Louis showed up, making for a fantastic, trio of independent singer-songwriters to kick start what would become a major entertainment innovation in an area taking off as a result of much-needed road and bridge infrastructure expansion.

Pony-tail-wearing, hard-singing Jay Hawkins is the classic honky-tonk entertainer; and his addition to the Flora-Bama shortly after Ken Lambert, helped create the special musical experience that all Flora-Bama patrons have come to know and love and expect through the years. Jay's voice is quintessential American country with a flair for the upbeat and raunchy. He has penned a number of original, memorable tunes through the years, including the fan favorite, "Dead Armadillo," which has received a modicum of commercial and folk success.

Jay is a kind fellow, and one can tell that he still greatly enjoys his job entertaining at the Flora-Bama, as his enthusiasm for the stage and the music, is evident. Jay told me that when he first hit the scene at the Flora-Bama he and Ken and Jimmy were really hitting on all cylinders.

"Nobody had ever seen or heard anything like us. We were really something. Word traveled fast and soon we had a huge following—and the people just kept on coming. People started calling me a 'honky-tonk' musician. One night, Joe came up to me. He was serious. He said, 'Don't go making my place a honky tonk club.' I just figured it was already too late."

Today, the Flora-Bama is known affectionately by many worldwide as one of the "Last great American honky-tonk roadhouses," a moniker it proudly resembles, as its definition applies.

Jay truly loves living life on the island, the place he has called home for over 30 years. "When you cross that bridge at Perdido Pass, it's like entering paradise," he said.

The story goes that Joe met Jimmy Louis while he was playing music on his birthday. Joe said that he went to see Jimmy play in Destin at the advisement of a friend. Predictably, Jimmy got drunk that night and wowed everyone with a fantastic performance. In fact, since it was his birthday, he even mooned the crowd. Joe explained that he hired Jimmy on the spot, and that he "Had to have him."

Fellow Louisiana musician and Flora-Bama regular, Johnny Barbados of the Lucky Doggs, said of Louis, "The level of output Jimmy Louis gives during a performance is amazing. He gives everything he has into each performance."

Jimmy Louis is a unique individual. During the season he works at a boat yard in Josephine, Alabama, across Perdido Bay, where he moors a little yawl named Desiree in the ever-popular indoor-outdoor, institutional haunt, Pirate's Cove. Jimmy also works on other boats there, repairing, sanding and painting them while he simultaneously writes songs. He said that he often writes songs while he's busy working on the boats, and that he finds the labor and the environment therapeutic; and interestingly, most conducive for songwriting.

"Everybody's free in Josephine at the Pirate's Cove," said Louis.

And he's right.

Pirate's Cove is one of the more interesting, off-the-beaten-path, must-see area spots. It is located north of the Flora-Bama on the Alabama shore of Perdido Bay. Unfortunately, it is easier to get there by boat than it is by automobile, as it is only a ten or fifteen minute boat ride from Old River near the Flora-Bama. By car it will take you 45 minutes, as you have to go east all the way around the periphery of Perdido Bay and then west down Highway 98 in Florida, and then Alabama, to get there.

Pirate's Cove is like a cousin of the Flora-Bama in look and feel. Possessing the same loveable, makeshift, ramshackle, driftwood and tin roof ambiance, it is also a popular live music venue. Furthermore, they sell their own potent brand of bushwhacker and are known for some of the best greasy cheeseburgers on the planet. Pirate's Cove is also a popular prop stop for boats, sailboats and jetskis, as on weekends during the summer months it is always a beehive of water craft activity. Also, Pirate's Cove is a dog lover's paradise. A hand-written placard marks the entrance to the establishment. Resting above a large, five-gallon clear plastic container of water marked 'for dogs not feet' it reads: "A Baldwin County ordinance prevents the presence of dogs in food-serving establishments. TOO BAD DOGS CAN'T READ."

Despite his laid-back nature, Jimmy Louis is serious about his craft, and has been for over thirty years.

"I'm a songwriter. It's a wide-open thing," he said. "Joe gave me a venue and a place to do my craft. He told me, 'I'll pour the whiskey. You play the music."

Jimmy explained how things were in the beginning.

"Ken Lambert was puttin' em to sleep and I was wakin' em up! And Joe was selling whiskey."

Joe noted that Jimmy should have long ago become a household name in country music. "Jimmy would have been world-famous but has never worried about business or being a star. He has actually turned down large record deals, not wanting the trouble it brings."

"I had money. All it did was confuse me," explained Louis.

Although he no longer does, for nearly a decade Jimmy spent four months of every year during the offseason in the Bahamas.

"Not many millionaires can do that. He knew what he was doing and he still knows what he is doing," remarked Joe about the way Louis approaches life.

Louis added that he misses his former annual excursions.

"I want to go back to the places I used to spend a year in, and spend five years."

***

To understand the full story of the beginnings of the Flora-Bama, and its eventual remarkable success as a universally known beach haunt specializing in daily live music and fun, you need to know about Outlaw country music. Ken Lambert, Jay Hawkins and Jimmy Louis in many ways personified (and still do) this loveable rogue subgenre of country that evolved across America during the late 1960's, and continued in the Deep South well into the early 1980's.

Outlaw Country or simply "Outlaw Music," was originated by rebel artists like Mickey Newbury, Johnny Cash, Waylon Jennings, Merle Haggard, David Allan Coe, Willie Nelson, Kris Kristofferson, Hank Williams, Jr. and Billy Joe Shaver. The reason for the new musical tack was because Nashville's recording gatekeepers, the former all-knowing kingmakers, like producer Chet Atkins—who were wholly responsible for the accepted "Nashville Sound," had for far too long tried to pigeonhole artists into conforming to their own narrowly-defined brand of traditional country music. Artists weary of Nashville's vice-like grip on their creative license naturally sought an abrupt change, and in that rebellious, innovative vein, the Outlaw Country Music movement was born.

 The roots of the outlaw movement can be traced all the way back to the 1950's and Elvis Presley's bluesy covers of tunes that were formerly country music standards. But, an even larger shift occurred when Waylon Jennings secured his own recording rights, and began the larger, climactic trend of overtly bucking the established Nashville sound.

The 1960's was a decade of enormous social change. This ideological upheaval was reflected in the musical revolution of the time. Rock N' Roll icons like the Beatles and the Rolling Stones bravely cast off the traditional role of the recording artist. Instead, they began writing their own material; they had real creative input in their albums; and they refused to conform to what mainstream society and music aficionados demanded of their former country musicians.

During this same time, country music was steadily regressing into a formula-driven genre—much like it is today; which appeared to offer the Nashville musical establishment what it wanted. However, this apparent safer, risk-free approach produced the kind of music that was completely unappetizing to the fickle palate of the growing counter culture movement. While thereafter Nashville continued to be the focus of mainstream country music, other creative musical centers like Lubbock, Tulsa, Austin, Bakersfield, California and yes—in Perdido Key at the Flora-Bama, were thriving.

The success of this new, exciting songwriting genre and music trend returned a much-appreciated rawness and vitality to what was most often simply labeled as "country." The newer, edgier songs produced during this time were about drinking, druggin', hard-working men and otherwise, fallible honky-tonk heroes. The fresh music was much more like ever-changing Rock N' Roll, and as a result it was much more upbeat and alive. Fans loved it.

From the beginning, Jimmy Louis has repeatedly proclaimed that he was never the Nashville type, and that he really wasn't cut out for the recording industry, either, for that matter. The Flora-Bama provided, he said, the perfect venue at the perfect time for him and Jay and Ken; as they were outlaws by nature, if not also by name.

In her book titled, *Jookin*, scholar Katrina Hazzard-Gordon aptly defined the American Honky-Tonk as "a rough establishment, one located mainly in the Deep South, one that serves alcoholic beverages to a working-class clientele. Further, honky tonks sometimes also offered dancing to piano players or small bands, and were sometimes also centers of prostitution, and that 'the name itself became synonymous with a style of music. Related to the classic blues in tonal structure, honky-tonk has a tempo that is slightly stepped up.'"

One of the early things Joe did to help out his working musicians was to provide a piece of land across the street from the Flora-Bama where the artists could park their RV's and campers. This lot, known affectionately as "Boys' Town," is where many of the Flora-Bama's steadier musicians and many other wayward, reveling souls have crashed and slept throughout the many years of the Flora Bama's modern operation.

According to musician/author Larry Strickland, there have been countless bonfires and parties held there into the wee hours of the morning; adding that it was not uncommon to routinely "watch the sun rise with a buzz." Obviously, Boys' Town holds a special place in the hearts of Larry and all the other musicians and support staff who shared time there working their dream gigs at the world-famous Flora-Bama.

***

Joe often talks about the simpler times that were his early days at the Flora-Bama. He reminisced about that second summer on the island—the summer of 1979—with great nostalgia.

"It was the summer of 1979, right before Hurricane Frederick ravaged the gulf coast and completely opened up this entire area to condo development. It was a warm summer night. I remember early on seeing that it was a clear night and that the moon was exceptionally bright. But, we were fairly busy, and as a result I was having fun with the customers, as usual, and didn't really pay much attention to what was going on outside. Around 9:30 p.m. or so, somebody came running from the beach into the bar. Back then we did not have a convenient boardwalk leading to the water. There was only soft sand, so it took longer to walk or run to the surf.

"The guy was breathing heavily and pleaded with me to go back with him to the water to see how beautiful it was at the beach. He was wildly enthusiastic, to the point that I couldn't say no; so I followed him. As we neared the water I saw how bright the night sky was. The moon appeared larger than normal, like a piece of cheese, and it was as clear a night as I had ever seen. More remarkable, at the water's edge, about ten yards out into the gulf, was a phosphorescent glow that I will never forget. The abundant phosphorous in the water had formed a mysterious green-lit glow, making for an unbelievable sight along the water line as far as the eye could see toward the east or the west. It was surreal.

"My friend and I quickly ran back to the Flora-Bama. Upon our return I got on stage between songs and commandeered the microphone. I told everyone in the bar—about two or three hundred people I'd guess—that they had two choices: 1) they could go home; or 2) they could come skinny dipping with the rest of us in the Gulf of Mexico. I explained that I would be providing the beverages.

"Minutes later, after grabbing several cases of cold beer, about a hundred or so of us jettisoned our clothes, and were innocently naked, enjoying a beautiful night, skinny dipping and chicken fighting in the surf like giddy school children. It was wonderful, and I can still remember the way the water strangely glowed that beautiful summer night."

Old timers at the Flora-Bama confirmed this story. Several told me that for the next couple of days people returned to reclaim their clothes they had gladly left at the beach that starry night.

***

Despite its historical whims and fascinations, life on the Key traditionally moves at a blissfully slow, relaxing pace. I spent about a week or so at the penthouse atop the Phoenix in Orange Beach. Although it certainly wasn't beach weather, I enjoyed the time spent with my new musician friends. In a whirlwind Joe introduced me to everyone around the Silver Moon and the Flora-Bama. I met all the regulars and many, if not most of the musicians who regularly played. It was quite a clip those first few, fun-filled, fascinating days. Everything was so new and exciting.

In late January Joe and I attended the annual Chili Bowl Cookoff amidst several hundred reveling snowbirds. Snowbirds through the years have become a welcome source of winter business for the Flora-Bama. Days later, we participated in the 2010 Perdido Key Mardi Gras Boat Parade, along with Sandy Laird and a few of the other regulars who frequent the Flora-Bama. Everyone except me wore a pirate-themed Mardi Gras costume onto the festively decorated, mid-sized fishing vessel. Joe conveniently forgot to tell me I needed to wear one. In fairness to him, he probably did, but I may have been, at the time, a bit weary, and thereby challenged to remember—which was a certain anomaly, as I am known to remember well. Joe even commented on my uncanny ability to always recall things.

"You have a pornographic memory," he quipped.

"Thank you. I resemble that," I responded and laughed.

As I recall, that mid-morning I was given some makeshift garb—a pirate's hat, an eye patch and some colorful scarves—along with an ice cold beer, to make me look more presentable for throwing worthless plastic beads to the fawning locals, snowbirds and curious international tourists who lined the waterway banks like seagulls seeking stale bread crumbs.

It turned out that Sandy Laird and I shared the same birthday, February 9th. She and Joe and I enjoyed birthday cake—candles and all, at the Silver Moon on the evening of our birthday. I turned forty. Sandy told me she had long quit counting.

After the deeply Southern, Pagan ritualistic festival of Mardi Gras was done, Joe encouraged me to find a place to stay in the area so that I could be around ground zero more, and to get to better know the community. I often call the Flora-Bama ground zero, as it is the certain epicenter of area fun. Joe strongly emphasized that I needed to spend some time in the area before I could effectively write about it. I wholeheartedly agreed with him. To gain true perspective takes time. I really needed to live in the area before I could thoughtfully write about it.

Joe suggested that I talk to Connie Blum, a former girlfriend of his, who worked as his personal business manager. Connie owned a lot on Perdido Bay on Innerarity Island that she purchased from Joe after Hurricane Ivan in 2004 razed the home he owned there. This was the home that singer-songwriter Ken Lambert lived in with Joe for some time during his hell-raising days as the Flora-Bama's pioneering, guitar-playing crooner. I never saw the place, as it was long gone by the time I arrived on the island, but it reportedly had numerous bullet holes in the walls that Ken had fashioned after a few of his legendary whiskey bouts.

Connie at the time used the Perdido Bay waterfront property as a modest income generator, charging rent for a trailer she parked where the house formerly stood. Connie also had two or three small storage structures and a working art studio there where she crafted beautiful glass art sculptures and large flat, multi-colored hanging pieces. Word was that her renter was leaving.

I got Connie's number from Joe and called her. I told her I would meet her at the lot to talk about possibly renting from her for a few months until I could get the book on the Flora-Bama written. I was a little leery of living, even temporarily, in a camper. I knew movie stars hung out in campers, but for some reason, the whole notion conjured blurry images of character Alonzo "Gonzo" Gates of the popular 1980's Trapper John, M.D., T.V. series. He lived in a broken-down R.V. in the hospital parking lot. Nevertheless, I really didn't want to spend too much money on a place, as money was tight, and from what Joe said, her lot was in a good spot. The camper idea was a definite alternative to renting a nearby condo, and it would give me a real taste of what Joe called, "Island life."

I floated the idea of getting a camper to a couple of my friends, arguing passively what I had pondered, that "Movie stars often hang out in trailers." One friend admitted as much without saying anything. The other, obviously the better friend of the two, retorted, "Yeah, but they go home to mansions."

Connie's property actually was in a great location, off of Bob-O-Link Street on Innerarity Point, a mere block away from Hub Stacey's on the Point, at 5851 Galvez Road on the Intracoastal Waterway. The place was also just down the street from the thirty-year old Innerarity landmark, The Point Restaurant, and about a ten-minute ride east from the Flora-Bama. Like the grand forerunner, the Flora-Bama, both Hub's and the Point have regularly-scheduled live music for the full enjoyment of their patrons. This common element of live music is an endearing, hallmark feature of the popular tourist destination area.

Hub's is a great little off-the-beaten path bar and grill on the Intracoastal Canal that opened in 2004. There is a popular public boat launch nearby, so the place stays pretty busy on weekends. Architecturally, much like Pirate's Cove, it appears to be a long lost cousin of the Flora-Bama, which makes it particularly loveable. At Hub's, like at McGuire's, there are dollar bills stapled everywhere across the restaurant's remaining open wall and A-framed ceiling space.

Joe and Sandy brought me and his niece, Heather Gilchrist, then a local sports anchor who has since moved on to a bigger market, to the landmark family restaurant, The Point, to enjoy a local delicacy—fried mullet. The Point is one of those places that inevitably grew to become a part of the community it serves. The Point Restaurant is a Perdido area mainstay. With a coin-operated jukebox for quieter times, an oyster bar with plenty of beers on tap and an outdoor courtyard with a stage, it has been a popular island respite revered by locals in the know for over three decades. And—they still serve mullet as a noted delicacy.

I am from Louisiana, where the mullet is largely considered a bait fish. Although it is just as plentiful in the Bayou State as it is in Florida and Alabama, people in Louisiana would rather eat other, more delectable trash fish, than mullet—like Choupique—which is a slimy, prehistoric Cypress Trout; or Garfish and Buffalo Carp.

So, when Joe said that he wanted to take me to The Point Restaurant "to enjoy fried mullet," I winced. Nevertheless, in keeping with the accepted "When in Rome" mantra, I politely bit my lip and went along.

The fried mullet at the Point really wasn't that bad—what little could be had by picking it slowly from the translucent, white skeleton that ran through the center of the thin strip of cooked white meat. It was a lot of work for a little bit of food, but it was a good, crispy appetizer, nonetheless. It wasn't bad at all.

We were the only customers at the Point that early March Sunday afternoon, quite an anomaly for an island institution that had been around for over thirty years. Joe asked to speak to the owner. He eventually emerged during our late lunch to confirm that sales had indeed been down. Business had not been this bad in years, he claimed. Joe introduced me to the aging proprietor and promised him that he would remind his friends to patronize their restaurant when they were in the area, as he understood well that times were tough.

About that time, in mid-March 2010, to stem the financial pressures a divorce often brings, I took a full-time job as a business writer and editor for a national healthcare company in Pensacola, Florida. At that juncture I lived in Fairhope, Alabama, which is an hour drive from downtown Pensacola, where my office is located. In Fairhope I was occupying a former rental property that my wife and I shared, the place I moved into after my separation. The lot on Bob-O-Link was about a half hour from downtown Pensacola where my new job was, so it was a likely prospect as a second island home, or camp, for me.

Joe's assistant, Connie Blum, and I met as planned at her property on Bob-O-Link on a navigable canal leading to Perdido Bay. She showed me the camper that some brave fellow was renting and living in at the time. It was for the most part unsettling, as the place was a wreck and the camper looked like it was old, generally unkempt and much smaller than I anticipated. I asked Connie if I could place my own camper on the lot, and she said yes. She also informed me how much the monthly rent was, and that it was due promptly on the first.

Connie is one of those lucky people who has been living and loving the island life for a long time. She landed a job at the Flora-Bama when she was 23 and never left. Connie is from nearby Pleasant Grove, Florida, where one of the bridges there is named after her father, Dub Blum. Somewhere along the line (no pun intended) she transitioned from Joe's girlfriend to his trusted confidante and business manager. The two to this day, share an interesting relationship.

Connie offered a half-hearted explanation of it all, "At one point I remember that I was 53, Joe's girlfriend was 43, and Joe's daughter, Marjorie, was 33!" Connie recalled laughing out loud, trying to draw semblance to it all.

I talked to Connie for a while about how I met Joe's brother, David and how he had the novel idea of me writing a book about Joe and the Flora-Bama. She broadly smiled as she listened intently. I explained that I was going to indeed write the book. When I was done explaining my intentions, she said matter-of-factly, with her hand on her hip, still beaming, through gleaming white teeth, "Honey, I can assure you—this is going to change your life! Get ready! You will never be the same!"

I really didn't know what to think about her comment.

On *Craig's List* I found a slightly-used 29-foot Skyline brand *Weekender* camper. The previously stored camper was immaculate inside and out, with all of the stickers still on the appliances, having only been used as a refuge of last resort by the former owner and his elderly relatives during the powerful hurricanes of Katrina and Rita four years earlier. After making a fair deal with the owner, I had the camper delivered to the island. Once the power was connected and the air conditioner was humming, I was pretty much set to begin my adventuring quest to write a book about the iconic Flora-Bama and its many fabled characters.

Things were looking good. I had a place to stay near The Line and close to my new job in downtown Pensacola. I was excited. Nevertheless, I thought more and more about what Joe said.

Like he suggested, I tried hard at the proper times, to become more useless. I began to have more fun—to do the types of things that I hadn't done since I was kid; things like kayaking, jet skiing, swimming, hiking the many area dunes and riding my bike. I was quickly meeting people, the many characters the Flora-Bama has to offer daily, as Joe called them; and as I pondered that first spring night before sleeping alone in the camper near the placid Perdido Bay, I wondered how much truth there was to what Connie Blum had told me while laughing—that "I would never be the same again."

Chapter Six
Laughter and Song

"He who loves not laughter, wine, women or song
—remains a fool his whole life long."

- Unknown

One of the many unique aspects of the Flora-Bama is that not only does it have great music—and all the wonderful characters who create and enjoy it—but it has attracted and maintained a fierce gaggle of giggle-producing crooners who passionately infuse song and laughter to produce what is always a memorable, joyous time. Laughter has been called the best medicine, and at the Flora-Bama it is doled out in liberal doses.

Before he succumbed to throat cancer in 2005, James Rushton "Rusty" McHugh, III was the Deep South's much funnier and talented version of Weird Al Yankovic—an insanely clever lyricist, drawing on the natural, satirical foibles of Redneck kind, and an equally talented singer and entertainer. "The Flora-Bama is a writer's paradise…there are more hooks coming out of that place," once said the departed McHugh.

Rusty was a great singer/songwriter if there ever was one, and he was as original as he was fun, bringing regular streaming tears of laughter to his adoring fans with notable numbers like, "Tequila Makes my Clothes Fall off," "I Never met a Bitch That Could eat so Much," and of course, "We all Love a Woman With a big ole' Ass," among many other laudable, laughable numbers like, "I saw your bra hanging in the Flora-Bama."

Interestingly, according to local legend, the Tequila tune was apparently somehow borrowed by Gary Hannan and John Wiggins and recorded by Joe Nichols under the slightly different title, "Tequila Makes Her Clothes Come Off." In 2005, the latter version rose to the top of Billboard's Hot Country Chart. Joe told me that Rusty could have sued, but chose not to.

The story behind the song, according to Rusty, in an interview featured in the Flora-Bama documentary, "The Last Great American Roadhouse," by Alan Brockman, was that one mid-day at the Flora-Bama Rusty ran into one of the female Flora-Bama bartenders, who just happened to be nursing a hellacious hangover.

The dragging drink slinger informed Rusty, "Tequila makes my clothes fall off!" Rusty immediately replied, "Darlin' that's a song!" and like the good writer he was, proceeded to write it.

Another of Rusty's songs speaks to what he considered the good life, of having "A case of Old Milwaukee, an ugly woman and a shitty bag of pot."

Rusty commented on how enjoyable it always was to make fun of people through song.

"Nobody ever thinks you're singing about them," he said. "You see, we weren't singing about *you* bitches…we were singing about *them other* bitches…and that's okay."

Rusty reportedly once told a lively Flora-Bama patron, "We're screwing this cat, lady! Just hold the tail."

You can still buy Rusty's hilarious CD's at the Flora-Bama, inside the big tee shirt trailer out front running parallel to the beach highway.

I never saw Rusty McHugh play live and sing, as he passed away from cancer in 2005, but I have immensely enjoyed his music on CD, and on rare, vintage live video footage recorded at the Flora-Bama and the Silver Moon where he once regularly played. Joe made sure that I saw Rusty's performances.

Rusty McHugh was one-of-a-kind in that he would write songs about anything—and he often did. He is missed as a true Flora-Bama legend, as he made so many laugh and smile and have fun. However, his proud legacy of laughter and song has been passed on to the next generation of crooning comics working at the Bama, to guys like Jay Hawkins and Jack Robertson. Jack Robertson knew Rusty well. He told me that Rusty always wholeheartedly encouraged him to continue to write and sing funny songs.

Rusty McHugh spent his life writing, recording and playing music. Beginning with the Fish Camp Band in Georgia, he evolved enough as an artist to open for Johnny Paycheck. Rusty eventually moved to the Redneck Riviera, settling in the Destin and Panama City Beach areas before finally landing in Perdido Key where he found a second home at the loveable Flora-Bama.

Rusty spent the last 12 years of his life on The Line, gaining a huge following of faithful, laughing fans. Before Rusty passed, he and his wife, Millie, spent a week in Jamaica, a place that Rusty dearly loved. A day after he returned, on February 21, 2005, he passed away. He is gone but not forgotten by those who loved him and his unforgettable, hilarious brand of music.

***

Joe informed me in the middle of February that I needed to be at the Flora-Bama for the second annual "Big Earlvis" show, starring Jack Robertson, a.k.a. "Big Earl," whose show I had recently seen for the first time one Sunday afternoon under the tent stage. Understand that these are two completely different shows. Jack Robertson normally performs as himself, Jack Robertson, or under his regular stage nickname, "Big Earl." He only every once in a while dons the "Big Eearlvis" attire making himself look much like the former King of Rock N' Roll, Elvis Presley, did when he was on his unflattering, bloated, last performing leg.

I am a fan of Elvis Presley. I admire his once-enormous talent, charm and charisma—and especially his ability to connect with a crowd. Having said that, I don't think there is anything wrong with what Jack does, because I believe wholeheartedly that if Elvis was alive today, he would laugh right along with us at "Big Earlvis," the quintessential Redneck Elvis imitation.

Like many of the artists who regularly perform at the Flora-Bama, Jack Robertson is a character. However, in Jack's case, the loosely descriptive term is a vast understatement. Jack is a rare blend of laughs and smarts who has a comedic Star Trek mentality in that he regularly goes "Where no man has gone before," in terms of act content. He is fearless.

Jack reportedly has a day job working in the health care business. He teaches good Southern folks how to work an ultrasound machine, which is equally noble and honest. However, on a handful of selected evenings each month Jack sheds the lackluster modus operandi of working stiff and becomes a bona fide State of Arkansas-born musical experiment, performing at the world-famous Flora-Bama to an always lively crowd.

By day Robertson may be an unassuming, mild-mannered medical teaching professional, but on performance nights he's one of the louder, raunchier and certainly funnier musical acts you'll find at the Flora-Bama—or anywhere in the United States of America, for that matter.

Jack has cleverly infused with song his unique brand of Southern digression, giving innovative, musical life to thoughtful creations such as:

1. Made Love to Your Mother

2. No one can Make Love Like my Sister can

3. Loving on a Chicken at the Motel 6

4. Chocolate City Blues

5. Old Cowpoke Pokin' an old cow

6. Beauty is a Light Switch Away

7. Making Love in the Flora-Bama Parking Lot

8. Eatin' Corn and Watching Porn

9. Titties Full of Beer

10. Poontang on a Pontoon

Now, this certainly isn't a Top Ten arrangement of Jack's prolific work as an artist—he just came out with a greatest hits compilation—but it's nonetheless a fine representation of his unique talent and insatiable penchant for belly laughs.

Jack's act is made even more enjoyable by the presence of one Cathy Pace, a veteran Flora-Bama bass player and singer who complements him well. Cathy also plays bass for Jezabel's Chill'n, another Flora-Bama band that is a mainstay in the weekly live music lineup (Larry Strickland plays with Jezabel's Chill'n too). Cathy is as sweet and dedicated as she is funny and talented. She and Jack consistently show up strong and make everyone in the crowd laugh. In many ways, they personify the spirit of the Flora-Bama, as they always ensure that everyone in attendance laughs and has a good time—even the most ornery and miserable of patrons will inevitably chuckle hard. They are hilarious.

The Big Earlvis Show began in 2009. It was an immediate hit, drawing rave reviews from legions of raucous rednecks across the Deep South. Jack, never to shy away from a good gag or gig, decided to step it up in 2010. He made an emphatic statement. What I saw that Saturday night in February 2010, will be forever etched in my fading memory banks.

***

Days before the show Joe told me I needed to get there early, that it was a standing-room-only event. Slated to start at 7:00 p.m., I was urged to arrive no later than 6:30 p.m. in front of the expanded tent stage, where Joe said he'd save a spot for me. I didn't get there until just before seven, but apparently the extra preparations put in by Big Earlvis and the supporting cast pushed the start of the show back a few minutes, so I was good.

I parked behind the Silver Moon and hustled across the beach highway in a bee's line toward the side entrance to the Flora-Bama. The Bama was undergoing major construction at the time. They were building the new balcony and stage areas, and the entrance seemed to never be in the same spot from week to week.

As I crossed the asphalt, beach roadway I saw a young guy in his twenties, looking like a modern beatnik of sorts, wearing a broad white sandwich board painted with large, thick black lettering. He wore a non-descript blue baseball cap and dark sunglasses. His board on one side read: "Respect the King!" The reverse read, "Don't Mock the King!"

I stopped dead in my tracks. I was incredulous.

"You're kidding, right?" I implored.

"Respect the King! Don't mock the King!" he yelled, unfazed. He loudly repeated.

"Respect the King! Don't mock the King!"

"Hey man—you're kidding, right?" I asked again.

He stopped what he was doing and looked at me funny.

"Is this for real?" I asked.

"Whattayou mean?" he answered, matter-of-factly with a straight face.

"So you are protesting this event?" I asked.

"We have to show some respect, man!" He said with emphasis, shrugging his weighted shoulders, simultaneously lifting his hands unsuccessfully into the air, as they were blocked by the straps holding up the large, bulky sign.

He had a point, I thought. Before Elvis became an obese drug-addicted sloth he was a revolutionary cultural icon and entertainer. He probably did deserve better.

As I contemplated his noble crusade, he obviously lost his wits.

"Okay, okay, it's a joke." He said, smiling ear-to-ear.

"They paid me to do this."

"They?" I questioned.

"Big Earlvis and the show."

I was had. He noticed, and broadly smiled again. I turned, without comment, and hustled into the Bama, wearing an anxious smile of my own.

The entrance to the Flora-Bama was on the left side near the tent stage. I entered and looked into the crowd. Joe was waiting for me on the front row like he said. The place was packed. I quickly realized it would be best to go through the back of the stage to get to him since I likely would have needed to grease myself to go the proper way and get through the reveling throng to where he was up front. With Joe's help in the form of a nod to the doormen, I slipped through a wide opening in the back of the tent near the makeshift entrance and walked right onto the stage. Joe quickly motioned me over. The place buzzed with excitement. You could tell something big was readying to happen—Big Earlvis, to be exact.

Joe handed me a cold beverage and we surveyed the building scene. A raucous, billowing crowd had arrived under the tent as Rhonda Hart, Leeann Creswell and Cathy Pace took the stage dressed as funky early 1970's backup singers. Their makeup appeared to have been scooped on and each wore flashy, sequin-filled, low-cut blouses, outrageous blonde, red and brunette wigs, high heels, fishnet black pantyhose, sunglasses, glitter and miniskirts. They looked great.

From the thick of the loud throng emerged a louder commotion. Six inebriated rednecks broke through a logjam of revelers with a cheap brown wooden coffin perched precariously on their shoulders. A couple of the bearers still had frozen bushwackers bearing straws in their hands. They headed quickly toward the stage. One of the guys stumbled and fell, temporarily burdening the remaining five pall bearers. The befallen gent gained his composure forthwith and resumed his duty, helping his cohorts lug the heavy cargo in a violent heave onto the makeshift stage.

With a loud thump the casket landed sideways onto the stage. There was momentary silence. Everyone in attendance stared at the lifeless, rectangular brown box. Several seconds later its lid opened unassisted. Big Earlvis, dressed in a sequined, white Elvis jump suit stuffed with a large pillow in the front, emerged, stumbled and then struggled like a Weeble Wobble, to his feet.

Large, dark sunglasses tilted precariously on his nose, much like the floppy, black pompadour wig did on the top of his head. As Big Earlvis's stammer subsided, and he found purchase on the center stage, someone handed him a wired microphone. The crowd raged with a cacophony of shrill, cackling laughs and shrieks.

"E! Elvis! I love you!" yelled one middle-aged woman trying her best to bull rush the stage past security. Another lady offered white laced panties. One even donated an expensive, over-sized, padded, metal-rimmed brassiere. A pair of tiny pink panties landed near Earlvis's shuffling feet, predictably catching the lazy eye of the rotund crooner. Then, in a surprise move, a middle-aged man successfully broke through the security line and rushed the stage. He was summarily apprehended by two security guards dressed like the Blues Brothers in dark fedoras and Ray-Ban sunglasses, lazily guarding the front of the stage. As the burly two wrestled the man away, he yelled, "Long live the King! Long live the King! Long live the King!" The place went nuts.

It was surreal. I turned to Joe amidst a cacophony of laughter and applause and commented, "Adults shouldn't be allowed to have this much fun."

He laughed heartily and confided.

"That guy who just rushed the stage owns 25 Sonic Drive-Ins in Mississippi."

"That guy?" I asked, motioning to where the man was before being apparently yanked from the crowd (I later saw him back where he was).

"Uh huh," Joe explained. "He's part of the act too. Just another character looking to have fun…you never know who you're going to see here. You just never know."

Big Earlvis wasted no time entertaining. He used a few choice expletives to introduce and endear himself to the crowd, and then began singing Elvis's many hit songs that made him a worldwide Southern American iconoclast: "Heartbreak Hotel," "Suspicious Minds" and "CC Rider," among others; and I am certain—that the King was rolling in his grave.

After the introductory numbers, Big Earlvis lovingly implored to the belly-laughing crowd, "Where's my beotches?"

Like clockwork, two women dressed in white nursing outfits with little white nurse hats emblazoned with a red cross and short matching mini-skirts, black fishnet stockings and pointed red high heels pranced onto the stage. The taller one held a large, dark blue bottle of Skyy Vodka on a platter. The much smaller of the two held a large jar of gummy bears that had a homemade sticker on the side that read "PILLS." Also, it is well worth adding that the pill-bearing nurse was a blonde-haired midget—one with an obviously fantastic sense of humor.

Earlvis again acknowledged their presence with a perfunctory, "My beotches" and grabbed his crotch and a handful of "pills" and ate them, washing them down with the "vodka," which was likely water. Or maybe it wasn't. I did not check. It made for pure satire, however. The crowd loved it, as they wildly cheered Elvis's renowned self-destructive behavior.

Earlvis even sprinkled in a few Jack Robertson originals like "Obama is White From the Waist Down," in between genuine Elvis songs. The avowed evening highlight was the unveiling of Jack's newest hit song, "Poontang on a Pontoon," which had quickly become the theme song of many local island dwellers. It was a fantastic show.

In fact, the show was such a hit Jack decided to take the following year off, so as to create a demand for the act through deliberate fan deprivation. However, this clever marketing decision by Jack pissed off many of the local regulars, who by January 2011, were pining for a repeat of the previous year's spectacle. It was also reported at the Silver Moon over the bar that Jack wanted a raise for doing the show, but was unsuccessful in his collective bargaining discussions with Joe. However, this was never confirmed and can really only be considered hearsay. It should nevertheless be noted that Jack later told me, "It sure is tough finding good midget help in this economy. Obama is freaking killing us!"

***

On March 11, 2010, the *Pensacola News Journal* ran on the top of its front page the following headline, "Owner of Iconic bar in the red." The front and center featured article began, "The majority owner of the Flora-Bama Lounge on Perdido Key has filed for personal bankruptcy, but expects the iconic lounge to survive."

The local newspaper story detailed the sheer depth of Joe's financial woes in an extremely embarrassing, and public way. It announced Joe's impending day in United States Bankruptcy Court in Pensacola on April 6, 2010, listing more than $37.8 million in unpaid debts resulting from his many varied real estate investments in condominiums and other developments gone bad.

Joe was quoted in the article, "I made a mistake investing in Escambia County and its real estate. The county has done little to encourage people to come and build here. It's just primarily that most people who have invested in America have been let down by their leadership in government at all levels from local, state and federal."

He added, "The sad thing is that you have someone who has grown up in the community and who has tried to do good things in the community. It is sad to me that I cannot meet my financial responsibility."

The News Journal piece noted that Joe's listed assets totaled $11 million, and that he would likely have to give the failed real estate properties back to the banks that financed them.

However, Joe's attorney, John Venn, clarified in the news article that Joe's assets were actually much more, after his majority stock ownership in the Flora-Bama was taken into consideration. The only apparent problem was placing a measurable value on the stock, as the popular business was mainly a cash one, and had never been fully appraised for such an unlikely, impromptu stock sale.

"It's a question of getting experts to look into them (the stock) and value them. The plan we would propose will provide for him (Joe) retaining his interest in Flora-Bama and paying his creditors out of income from it." Venn added.

When I read the front page article that morning I immediately felt for Joe. I knew that it was an extremely difficult time for him. It had been—ever since he had confided in his employees that he had no other choice but to file for bankruptcy. I had come into his life during a most turbulent time. It has often been said that a man's character is best judged in how he handles defeat, than rather how he handles success.

Failure is never easy. Losing is not fun. Losing your home and other valuables is unfathomable to most people, and in some respects can be considered the end game.

The article revealed just how big of a pinch Joe had found himself in. I sensed that losing the assets and his home were certainly tough. However, I also felt that among the things that remained in the balance, were those Joe was most proud of in life—his business reputation, and of course, his avowed life work—the revered Flora-Bama.

Later that afternoon, after I finished work and was back at the camper at the compound on Bob-O-Link, I ran into Connie Blum. I mentioned to her that I read the article about Joe's bankruptcy and that I felt terribly sorry for him. She knew all about the article, as she had, as usual, spent most of the day with Joe. She didn't say much about it, although I could tell it had affected her somber mood.

I had to press the issue. I asked, "Connie, do you think Joe is going to be able to save the Flora-Bama?"

In retrospect, I probably seemed a bit melodramatic. But, I had quickly grown to care about Joe. He is one of those types of people that you don't just like, but love. I hated to see everything he had worked for in his life—the wonderful Flora-Bama—go to a bunch of predatory, Pterodactyl lawyers and bankers.

In a most serious way, Connie looked at me and said, unnervingly, "They're gonna try and take it all, honey. One of these days, we're gonna wake up and it will all be down the river."

It was a chilling thought.

***

Later that evening I caught up with the popular singer/songwriter Sam Glass, in between music sets at the Flora-Bama. Sam is one of the area's mainstays, and is as likeable as he is talented and fun. A native of La Porte, Texas and a former Navy corpsman, Glass in appearance reminds one of a young Robert Redford, with piercing blue eyes and wavy, bleach-blond hair. Sam, who for a while lived on a sailboat moored in Perdido Bay, made his way to the Flora-Bama via Gilley's in Pasadena, Texas, where he got his start performing after his military discharge. Sam's mantra is as fun as his youthful countenance and smile: "Get some sand on it!" Sam told me that he felt for Joe, and knew that he was going through a tough time. After all, it was Joe who had given Sam and his players a regular gig as one of the Flora-Bama's house bands. Before he went back on stage, he left me with a poignant remark, given all that was transpiring in our part of the world.

"If Joe makes it, we all make it."

He was right.

Chapter Seven
Beach Polluter (BP)

"War is peace. Freedom is slavery. Ignorance is strength."

-George Orwell

While Joe was clamoring to save the Flora-Bama along with his business reputation in an already difficult tourism economy, things took an unsuspecting, unimaginable turn for the worst.

On April 20, 2010, British Petroleum, Halliburton & other misguided oil exploration subcontractors allowed the occurrence of one of the worst man-made oil spills in modern history. Apparently a single blowout protector on the rig failed to do its intended job, and as a result, jettisoned millions of gallons of unrefined crude oil into the theretofore gulf's foamy, turquoise waters.

It was later learned through a letter written from California U.S. House Representative Henry Waxman to BP Chief Tony Hayward, dated June 14, 2010, that Brian Morel, a BP drilling engineer, on April 14, 2010, just a week before the explosion that set off the spill, tellingly emailed a colleague that "this has been a nightmare well which has everyone all over the place."

Days after the accident, which occurred 50 miles off the South Louisiana coastline, it was embarrassingly revealed that other countries, like Brazil, require not one, but two blowout preventers, and that neither British Petroleum nor the United States Federal Government, had available adequate floating booms to contain the massive, growing slick.

Thanks to fortuitous headwinds, the huge, dark brown spill hovered offshore for almost three weeks before it finally began making its unavoidable approach to land along the Louisiana, Mississippi and Alabama coastlines during the first week of May.

The idiocy of the tragedy of the oil spill—eleven rig workers were tragically killed in the blast—was punctuated by a pathetic government response and an even more disappointing set of media coverage that virtually ended the area's annual lucrative summer tourist season.

The *Associated Press* sent a reporter, Bill Kaczor, to the Flora-Bama in late April to cover the spill's many deleterious effects. The reporter talked with more than one of the beach bar's workers, asking each about the oil spill and its apparent impact on the area. One of the bartenders gave the reporter what he wanted—a particularly juicy quote about the awful smell of the oil in the gulf. The bartender, after the fact, claimed he was misquoted.

> "Perdido Key, a Florida barrier island between Pensacola and the State of Alabama lined with sugar-white sand and studded with condominiums, could be the first place to be affected by the oil spill.
>
> "You could smell it, a real heavy petroleum base," said Steve Owensby, 54, a maintenance man at the Flora-Bama Lounge.
>
> The air later cleared, but Owensby's 28-year-old daughter, Stephanie, who tends a bar at the lounge, said some visitors had complained of feeling ill from the fumes.
>
> 'It's very sad because I grew up out here,' she said. 'I remember growing up seeing the white beaches my whole life. Every day I've been going to the beach ... a lot of people are out watching and crying.'"

The *Associated Press* ran the story May 5, 2010, and it was shortly thereafter picked up, along with the damaging quote, worldwide. The backlash from locals that read it was ire-filled.

Joe was terribly upset that one of his workers had possibly provided fodder for a "so-called" journalist, but he was equally if not more upset with the so-said journalist for writing the article the way that he did. This quote, according to Steve Owensby, never happened, so the entire episode—the article and its ugly aftermath, was nauseating for Joe, the Flora-Bama workers and the rest of the Gulf Shores, Orange Beach and Perdido Key communities.

"I was incensed because it appeared that the reporter came here with the intent to write a negative article. The other patrons he spoke to that day said nothing about the smell of oil. There was no oil on the beach and no fumes in the air. I was there." Joe emphasized.

In hindsight, the nausea over the journalistic snafu was understandable. Before the oil spill, the entire gulf coast business and tourism community was already nervous, worrying about the 2010 summer season's profitability; uncertainty was ubiquitous. The summers of 2008 and 2009 had been terribly disappointing sales-wise, as the economy was still badly reeling from the seemingly endless great recession.

Nevertheless, in late April, the entire resilient beach community was pining for a respectable increase in tourism and resulting spending. At the time there was still hope that things could improve. After all, a modest ten percent increase in sales would have been a huge boon to area businesses. But, like a thief in the night, British Petroleum—through extreme arrogance, greed and negligence—stole that last, remaining glimmer of economic hope from an already downtrodden lot. After April 20, 2010, and the subsequent tormenting weeks of helplessness, incompetence and inaction, hope was in shorter supply than a favorable press clipping stating truthfully that the spilled oil had not spoiled the Alabama-Florida gulf coast beach experience.

Neither BP nor the federal government was prepared to act with certainty and effectiveness in the wake of the gusher. Pandemonium reigned in the long weeks following the initial news of the massive environmental disaster. Because of this, the President of the United States, Barack Obama, encountered a growing backlash from those disgruntled with the lackluster public response.

In a *New York Times* article by Campbell Robertson and Eric Lipton titled, "BP is criticized Over Oil Spill, but U.S. Missed Chances to Act," it was clear that the federal bureaucracy had been slow to respond in the early days after the spill, and when it finally did, their response was as ineffective as it was disjointed.

In late May, the oil still gushed on the gulf floor at a rate of nearly one million gallons per day. After more than a month of unthinkable despair for gulf coastal residents, BP's Chief Executive Officer, Tony Hayward, visited beleaguered Venice, Louisiana, one of the closest cities to the spill's origin, to apologize for the prolonged disaster. In Venice, Hayward was asked pointedly by reporters what he would like to tell locals whose lives had been so adversely affected by the manmade catastrophe. His answer made history.

"The first thing to say is I'm sorry. We're sorry for the massive disruption it's caused their lives. There's no one who wants this over more than I do. *I would like my life back.*"

A spoken word has the same impact as an arrow sent or a bullet shot—you cannot get it back. The hurtful damage was quickly done. It was incontrovertible, and it outraged people everywhere. A few weeks later, in late July, the gaffe-prone Hayward was publicly fired from his high-profile position and reassigned to a project in the icy Russian heartland, after receiving a year's salary compensation package of $1.6 million and thereafter his annual pension of around $1 million. There was no mention of whether or not Mr. Hayward retained his many stock options and BP stock holdings.

About a week later, on June 8, 2010, as the crude continued to gush unabated deep on the gulf floor, an embarrassed and exasperated President Barack Obama stated that he wanted to know "whose ass to kick" over the oil spill, trying to somehow pressure BP to find a solution to the gushing well nearly a mile below the gulf's surface. In a subsequent cable television interview, President Obama also said that if Tony Hayward worked for him, "he would have fired him by now."

The latter comment by the President was an interesting one, especially considering the fact that during his brief tenure in the Senate (three years in Illinois) and while running for President he received a total of $77,051 in campaign contributions from BP. Barack Obama remains the top recipient of British Petroleum PAC and individual money (BP employees) over the past 20 years, according to United States federal campaign financial disclosure records.

On June 24, 2010, a newspaper article titled, "Stressed Boat Captain Commits Suicide" appeared in the *Los Angeles Times*. The West Coast newspaper piece reported on a Gulf Shores, Alabama charter boat captain, William Kruse, 55, who was found on his moored vessel with a gunshot wound to his head; a fired pistol was found nearby the decedent. Friends of Kruse said that he had grown increasingly despondent over the dismal environmental and financial situations brought about by the spill.

"How can you deal with watching the oil kill every damn thing you ever lived for in your whole life?" said Ty Fleming, Kruse's friend and co-worker. Kruse, like many former charter boat captains, had been hired by BP, along with his vessel, to engage in the massive cleanup aftermath.

As bad as the crude spill was on marine life and the economy, BP's unpopular decision to use nearly one million gallons of toxic dispersants to break down the oil—so it wouldn't have to eventually clean it up, proved to be equally unsettling

British Petroleum aggressively collected roughly a third of the world's available supply of dispersants, millions of gallons of it, and used them on the spilled oil. According to Environmental Protection Agency reports, the chemical BP chose to use, Corexit, was more toxic and less effective than other available dispersants.

An environmental report by Alex Seitz-Wald dated May 17, 2010, at *Thinkprogress.org* detailed that, "Of 18 dispersants whose use EPA has approved, 12 were found to be more effective on Southern Louisiana crude than Corexit, EPA data showed. Two of the 12 were found to be 100 percent effective on Gulf of Mexico crude, while the two Corexit products rated 56 percent and 63 percent effective, respectively. The toxicity of the 12 was shown to be either comparable to the Corexit line or, in some cases, 10 or 20 times less, according to EPA."

Further, the manufacturer of the dispersant, Nalco Company, was once part of Exxon Mobil Corporation. Nalco's leadership at the time included executives at British Petroleum and Exxon. A BP board member who served as a company executive for 43 years also sat on Nalco's board, meaning the chemical was created by the oil companies to sell to oil companies.

While the use of dispersants was an attempt to keep oil off the beaches and out of the wetlands, scientists worried that "the dispersed oil, as well as the dispersants themselves, might cause long-term detriment and harm to marine life."

Even Nalco admitted the chemicals posed "a moderate" environmental hazard. A Corexit product was used in the infamous Exxon Valdez oil spill cleanup in Alaska, and workers there suffered various health concerns, "including blood in their urine and assorted kidney and liver disorders."

As to be expected, BP, the corporation, quickly became synonymous with "Beach Polluter." On nearby State of Alabama Highway 98, which runs through Southern Alabama all the way through Florida, what was prior to the spill a BP gas station, quickly became a Shell Oil station—a staunch consumer backlash against the company's negligence in the spill and its subsequent failed plugging and cleanup effort. The owner of the gas station placed a bed sheet over the BP sign until the Shell sign was installed. Meanwhile, the oil continued to stain the gulf environment; and as it did, hope waned.

BP's engineers were baffled as to an answer; and it was apparent, even early on in the summer, that it was going to ruin the 2010 tourist season. As it turned out, the early unfair press coverage of the spill seemed to snowball across the Deep South and the rest of the country, forcing vacation goers to make alternate beach plans.

On Sunday, September 19, 2010, in a Washington Times article titled, "Cement Plug Permanently Stops Oil Spill," by Harry R. Weber, it was reported that the well, after five months of unabated gushing, was finally permanently sealed, after spewing more than 200 million gallons of crude. In an interesting aside, a 69-year old Boca Raton plumber, Leslie Goldstein, owner of the proprietorship, "Plumber I Am," immediately claimed that BP used his capping proposal based on basic fire hydrant technology—the same one that appeared on the July 16, 2010, front page of the Boca Raton, Florida Sun-Sentinel, to diffuse the billowing oil.

In August, BP, in an effort to make whole again what it irreconcilably broke, began writing compensatory checks from its $20 billion fund to those who filed loss claims through the Gulf Coast Claims Facility (GCCF), the entity it established to formally receive, verify and pay claims for loss of income related to the oil spill. Average payments to businesses and individuals averaged around $25,000. During the next five months the oil company received 481,000 claims from those asserting that they were adversely affected by the spill.

In January 2011, Kenneth Feinberg, the attorney tapped by BP to administrate the GCCF, issued a statement saying that nearly 7,500 of those said claims (1.5% of total claims) were believed to be fraudulent. Feinberg added that the known dubious claims were forwarded to the United States Justice Department for criminal investigation.

While the compensatory checks to individuals and businesses were helpful, many of the recipients never realized that they had to pay federal taxes on those monies, creating another unforeseen problem for the disaffected and the government. Further, while many of the claims were paid, more than half of them remained unpaid. In the State of Alabama, as of January 2011, more than 38,000 (57 percent of the state total) claims remained open and uncompensated, casting a huge shadow of doubt over the entire BP claims and compensation process.

Common stories of waitresses at local restaurants receiving $20,000 checks from BP for wages lost resulting from the spill, and fishermen with boats receiving hundreds of thousands of dollars for their cleanup work—many times more than what they regularly made fishing, created a veritable feeding frenzy for BP money, explaining the sheer number of excessive filed claims for damages. The term "spillionaire" was quickly coined, describing the many people who fortuitously found an unexpected monetary bounty from the man-made environmental tragedy.

The oil spill was so massive and covered such a large gulf area across three states that BP needed help with the cleanup. The easy answer was to hire fishermen and shrimpers and other seafood harvesters with watercraft and an acute knowledge of the area to assist in the assignment. Anyone with a licensed commercial vessel was urged to contact BP to get involved in corralling and collecting the spilled crude, and most of them did, as the money was just too good. Those fishermen who were able to get these special cleanup jobs were paid handsomely for their time and trouble—in some cases up to several thousand dollars per day.

Of course, most of the people who received money from BP deserved it; however, many who deserved it did not, creating divisions among those who rightfully and wrongfully received help--and those who didn't. Even more disconcerting was the fact that those with political ties monetarily fared the best in the spill aftermath.

In Saint Bernard Parish, Louisiana, documents revealed that companies with connections to local political insiders received lucrative contracts and thereafter billed BP heftily for every conceivable expense, often without adequate supporting documentation. One such subcontractor billed BP $15,400 per month to rent a generator that usually cost only $1,500 per month. Another firm billed BP over $1 million per month for land it was previously renting for only $1,700 per month. It was not the only reported incident of politicians taking unfair advantage of the unsuspected BP tragedy and subsequent cash-windfall. Alabama had its own political embarrassments.

***

The recession, the oil spill and the resulting bad press were devastating to the gulf coast economy. While BP clamored to infuse money into the cash-strapped region through compensatory checks for sustained wage and income losses, the Obama Administration ostensibly worked against the much-needed financial recovery.

On May 30, 2010, an oil spill-solution minded Barack Obama issued a knee-jerk, six-month deepwater gulf drilling moratorium policy, effectively

The early years with Joe Gilchrist (top left) goofing around, Pat McClellan and J. Hawkins and his band.

82

Joe at the old main bar.

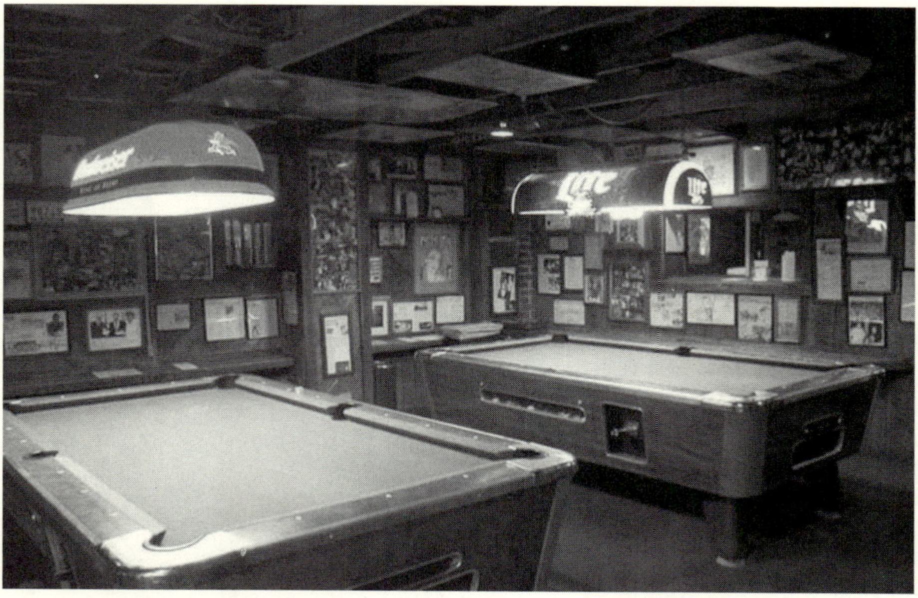

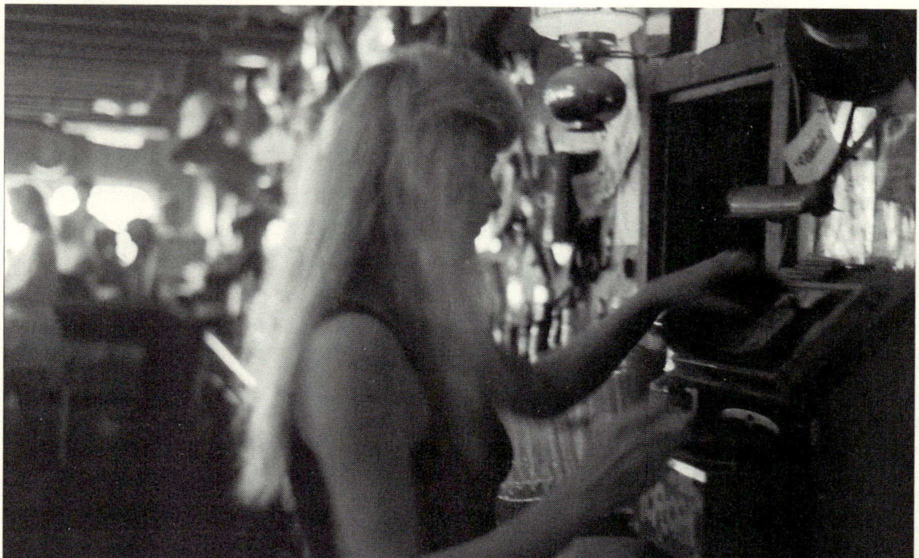

The old pool room and listening room.

Happy Birthday
Lite BEER
BARTENDERS DO IT STANDING UP!
OILWELL FIRES
NO. 1

The good ol' days...

OYSTERS
ON THE Half Shell

Coca-Cola
FLORA-BAMA
LOUNGE & PACKAGE

The old façade and package store.

Joe at the juke box.

Ivan's devastation of the Flora-Bama.

The Mullet Toss returns with a vengeance...

Seriously...

Pat (far left) at the Chili Cookoff

Writers' Crossing (left to right): Jody Payne, Chris Newbury, Beverly Jo Scott, Larry Jon Wilson, Bo Roberts, Cass Hunter, Sonny Throckmorton & Sam

Flora-Bama Bus

Polar Bear Plunge

Apollo Theatre

NYC Fire Station

Owners (from left to right): John McInnis, III, Joe Gilchrist and Bubba and Connie Tampary.

halting for at least a half year all drilling activity in the already beleaguered region. It had devastating consequences.

The moratorium on drilling in the Gulf of Mexico prevented 33 deepwater rigs in the Gulf of Mexico from operating. They were immediately shut down. This federal government action put many drilling jobs on the shelf, and consequently, many thousands of workers out of work and onto the already-swelled unemployment rolls.

The moratorium was short-lived, however. In late June 2010, a federal judge presiding over the Fifth U.S. Circuit Court of Appeals struck down what was typified as "a rash conclusion" by President Obama, that because one rig failed, others were also in immediate danger of failing.

Nevertheless, President Obama was undeterred. He simply issued another moratorium—saying through his Interior Secretary, Ken Salazar, on July 11, 2010, that a drilling reprieve was necessary to reduce the risk of another spill.

The first overturned moratorium applied to deep-water drilling in instances of over 500 feet. The new one was intended to be more comprehensive, yet was just as adverse in terms of its unintended economic impacts. While the President admittedly wanted to prevent another similar manmade environmental tragedy that killed eleven and wrecked the entire gulf coast economy, the drilling moratorium had many real, far-reaching, albeit unintentional, negative economic impacts.

Dr. Joseph Mason, partner at Empiris LLC, Moyse/LBA Chair of Banking at the Ourso School of Business at Louisiana State University, and Senior Fellow at the Wharton School, estimated the cumulative monetary loss in real wages, income and government tax revenues, in the six months after the moratorium's enactment, totaled $350 million per month, and over $2 billion overall.

Dr. Mason qualified his grim estimates with the following executive summary quote from his paper on the economic impacts of the Obama 2010 Drilling Moratorium:

"Halting all offshore deepwater drilling in response to a likely low-probability event serves neither to address the root causes of the accident, nor to aid in the economic rehabilitation of the Gulf region. Indeed, a moratorium on offshore drilling would result in billions in additional lost economic activity in the Gulf."

Chapter Eight

The Mullet Toss

"By culture we mean all those historically created designs for living, explicit and implicit, rational, irrational, and non-rational, which exist at any given time as potential guides for the behavior of men."

-Clyde Kluckhohn & William H. Kelly

It has been said that tradition does not graduate, that it does not ever leave the institution it embodies. One of the things Joe Gilcrhist and his initial partner Pat McClellan have done so well at the Flora-Bama that has undoubtedly contributed to their ongoing success is to create and sponsor a series of annual events, or institutional traditions, that keep people coming back in seasonal droves to the iconic beach bar. They include, but are not limited to (In chronological order over the year): The Polar Bear Dip, The Chili Bowl Cookoff, Mardi Gras weekend, Mullet Toss, Memorial Day, The Fourth of July Weekend, Labor Day, the Mullet Triathlon and the Songwriter's Festival in November.

The Flora-Bama has through the years sponsored a variety of musical, semi-athletic and athletic events. Each of these planned spectacles is great fun and always raises money for local charities. Undoubtedly, the most famous, or infamously popular of these planned festivities on the calendar is the Annual Interstate Mullet Toss, also known as the "World's Largest Beach Party," or by what comedic crooner Jack Robertson loves to metaphorically call—"Breast Fest."

Joe and Pat wanted an event to fill a relatively slow part of the calendar with something fun to do. So, on the last April weekend of every year since 1984, beach revelers from across the country and the globe have converged on the gritty ivory strip behind the Flora-Bama to compete against others throwing a wet mullet from the strict confines of a 10-foot diameter circle inside the

State of Florida into the air across the line into the neighboring State of Alabama. For paying for the opportunity to throw the mullet and compete for prizes and bragging rights, each contestant receives an official event tee shirt, and the tingling satisfaction of knowing that they helped raise money for a local charity.

According to Joe, long-time Flora-Bama Musician Jimmy Louis was the brain trust behind this fishy movement. Back in 1984, Jimmy mentioned to Joe that he had witnessed a cow patty-throwing contest while he was playing the rural Texas honky tonk circuit. Joe figured that throwing a mullet was no worse than throwing a cow patty, and alas, another great Flora-Bama event or tradition, was born; thereby demonstrating perfectly the South's penchant for zaniness and the infinite ability of its people to throw a good party.

Jimmy Louis explained how the idea for the popular event entered his creative consciousness. "The idea came to me in a fit of narcosis...I got stoned one night and thought it up. It was a dream...and like most good things, it just happened."

The inaugural Mullet Toss was held at the Flora-Bama's Fourth of July celebration in 1984. Now held earlier in the spring, it's one of the panhandle's biggest events, drawing annually over 20,000 people who come to witness the average tossing of more than 2,000 fish across the state line. However, folks go to the Mullet Toss for more than just fish chunking.

They go for the sights, as there are many sculpted, bare-chested men and equally scantily clad, toned, bronzed women in their ever-shrinking suits, which precede a well-attended, ultra-competitive string bikini contest held on a walkway stage underneath a large outdoor tent. Because of this, the Mullet Toss can and will often be a voyeur's as well as an exhibitionist's dream. For many years running, local Baldwin County (Foley) resident and former Alabama quarterback Kenny "The Snake" Stabler honored the occasion by serving as a Celebrity Mullet Tosser. About the same time, according to Joe, the starting quarterback for the New York Giants, Richard Todd, also came and visited the Flora-Bama with some frequency, and like Kenny, was a nice guy.

Kenneth Michael Stabler, a native of the nearby "Forward City" of Foley, Alabama, is a living legend of the Deep South if there ever was one. Born on Christmas Day in 1945, Kenny Stabler was not only a football star at the University of Alabama under venerable Bear Bryant from 1964 to 1967, but with the Oakland Raiders as well, winning Super Bowl XI with them in January, 1977.

Veteran Journalist Eddie Curran aptly noted in a 1992 *Mobile Press-Register* article about the Snake, "Few of us have been reprimanded, then praised, by Bear Bryant, won a Super Bowl, and/or partied with the Oakland Raiders and bikini-clad women while sipping cold beer for breakfast in a boat going 85 mph under or in proximity to the Alabama point bridge."

Local legend has it that Stabler, during his glorious football-playing days at nearby Foley High School, just off highway 59 South headed to the beaches, was quite the ruffian. I have been told by more than one who knew him back then that he loved to drive his Volkswagen Beetle, painted in the Foley Lion colors of navy blue and white, down to the Hangout, located at the "T," where State Highway 59 meets the beach road at the gulf, and fight any and all comers.

"Kenny loved to drink beer and fight," one undisclosed, former Fairhope Pirate the same age as Kenny, told me. "It was always the Fairhope and Robertsdale guys against the Foley guys, but it was serious stuff, and the local cops were always chasing Kenny in that Volkswagen of his."

The first Mullet Toss wasn't as auspicious as everyone hoped, as bad weather foiled the inaugural event. Nevertheless, through the years it has become one of the most popular of the many fun and zany Flora-Bama calendar dates. Locals still consider and treat the event like a national holiday.

Although it has fins, the mullet is hardly aerodynamic. Further, it is slimy, which makes throwing it particularly difficult. The current amateur Mullet Toss record is held by Josh Serotum, who in 2004 tossed an obviously streamlined mullet an amazing 189'8" in his preliminary toss and 174' 3" in his final toss. While tossing techniques are various and sundry, the best method appears to be folding the fish and chunking it overhand like a baseball, or football—or a javelin.

In 2009, Roald Bradstock, of Hertford Heath, England, the former 1986 World Record holder (81.74 meters) in the javelin, threw the mullet 169 feet 9 inches, some 20 feet short of Serotum's record.

"I threw it too high," Bradstock said. "I know I could throw it (the mullet) farther, but I think that once is enough." Bradstock did better his cell phone-throwing world record that day, sending his communication device 211 feet eight inches. Bradstock is also an artist who depicts sport. His work can be found in the extensive sport art gallery in Daphne, Alabama at the United States Sports Academy.

Despite repeated attempts to have Serotum's record sanctioned by *Guinness' Book of World Records*, the world record sanctioning body refuses to recognize this amazing human feat of strength and skill, even though it oddly recognizes the sanctioned throwing records of cell phones, iPods and egg tosses.

***

The 2010 Mullet Toss, much like the first in 1984, was sullied on Friday and Saturday by torrential rains, keeping many from making their annual skin pilgrimage to the Deep South's ivory hot coast. However, Sunday turned out to be a crisp, beautiful, blue bird day, drawing many remaining voyeurs and spectators, and of course an enthusiastic bevy of late mullet toss participants, myself included. It was my second time throwing fish, having done so the previous day.

Despite Saturday's cloudy, intermittent rainy weather—it wasn't as bad as Friday, and therefore I still made it out to the beach to serve as an Honorary/Celebrity Mullet Tosser at Joe's side.

When I arrived Saturday morning on the baby powder sand under graying skies I saw Joe standing with a man I recognized as the University of Alabama's former basketball coach, Mark Gottfried. It was Gottfried's turn at tossing the fish.

Lisa Faust, a Flora-Bama member and regular, was there with a plugged microphone connected to a loud amplified speaker to greet each contestant and to explain the rules.

"First, you have to take your shirt off," she said with a smile, anxiously pulling Gottfried's shirt off of his back. Gottfried blushed amidst a smattering of cat calls.

"Then, you have to clean the sand off of your hands by dipping them in the water," she added. Faust pointed to the large plastic bucket of salted ice water and dead mullet. The dead fish with clouded eyes stared motionlessly into the misty, pale sky.

"Now pick your mullet," she said to a still red-faced Gottfried, who nonchalantly grabbed, folded and tossed a fish from the designated circle like so many before and after him. The fish sailed from Florida into the great State of Alabama.

"Now go get your fish!" Faust yelled.

Gottfried, not to disappoint, begrudgingly sauntered across the sand and retrieved the half-frozen flyer from three scantily-clad girls wearing colorful string bikinis, dropping it back into the ice bucket upon return before again donning his shirt.

Just before Gottfried threw his fish a conspicuous fellow caught my eye. A really muscular dude about six foot three stood alone behind the crowd gathered around the throwing circle. He smoked a Marlboro Light, and had nearly used it completely, dragging on the unlit filter. It was cashed; but he pulled on it, nonetheless. Finally, he realized it was spent, and flicked it into the sand beneath his feet, stamping it out in the process.

Lisa Faust's voice on the microphone returned.

"John Rocker, you're next to throw."

"I knew the bowed up guy looked familiar!" I thought. I am an avid sports fan, and I recognized Rocker as the former big league closer who was known for his controversial, politically incorrect remarks about New Yorkers not speaking English. Despite all the hype surrounding his personal opinions, I always liked him as a fierce, exciting major league competitor.

For a story published in the January 2000 issue of *Sports Illustrated*, Rocker made a number of candid comments regarding his experiences in New York City. Specifically, he answered a question on whether he would ever consider playing for the New York Yankees or the New York Mets. Rocker's response was accused of being racist, homophobic, xenophobic and sexist.

> "I'd retire first. It's the most hectic, nerve-racking city. Imagine having to take the 7 Train to the ballpark looking like you're riding through Beirut next to some kid with purple hair, next to some queer with AIDS, right next to some dude who just got out of jail for the fourth time, right next to some 20-year-old mom with four kids. It's depressing... but the biggest thing I don't like about New York are the foreigners. You can walk an entire block in Times Square and not hear anybody speaking English. Asians and Koreans and Vietnamese and Indians and Russians and Spanish people and everything up there. How the hell did they get in this country?"

In Rocker's book, *Scars and Stripes*, published in 2011, he alleged that the notion of 'free speech' has unfortunately become more of an oxymoron than an absolute.'" Further, he pontificated on the unintended, adverse consequences, like censorship, that political correctness has had on free speech. In his book he does admit, however, that his comments about New Yorkers, in the context that they were reported by *Sports Illustrated,* were "cold, heartless…and mean."

Lisa Faust gleefully stripped the sculpted, former pro athlete of his white cotton tee shirt, which drew another, healthier round of cat calls from the watching crowd. Rocker, like Adonis, rippling with muscles, carefully selected his favorite fish. As he grabbed and folded it, someone in the crowd yelled, "Hey John! No sand! If you use sand on your hands you're cheatin! No sand, John! No cheatin!"

Rocker, the major league veteran, without a moment's hesitation, quipped in a deep, baratone voice that everyone in the vicinity could clearly hear, "If you ain't cheatin,' you ain't tryin!'"

Rocker's comedic punch drew raucous laughter and applause from the nearby throng. He quickly wound up and threw his mullet, but was premature in his release, causing the fish to fly higher and not farther; forcing it mainly up into the air. The final tally on the distance thrown was a mere 96 feet, which was more than disappointing. Former Alabama receiver Tyrone Prothro, whose playing career was ended by a devastating compound leg fracture against the Florida Gators, earlier tossed the mullet nearly 140 feet. The day's top throw was over 180 feet.

After Rocker threw his dead fish, my name was called by Joe, not Lisa, meaning I was allowed to throw the mullet while wearing my shirt. I picked a fish, folded it and chunked it as far as I could. The end result was 98 feet eight inches—two feet better than a former pro baseball player. I was proud—but I still had to run and get my fish.

Rocker, despite his edgy reputation, was a great sport that afternoon, staying afterward to sign autographs and tee shirts for children and fans. I later learned that he and I weren't the only honorary celebrity mullet tossers there that zany, overcast afternoon.

After Rocker and I threw fish, Joe introduced two local political dignitaries, Escambia County (Florida) Commissioner Gene Valentino and Mobile County (Alabama) Commissioner Stephen Nodine. Joe explained on the microphone to the crowd that the two would be throwing and representing each state they served, Florida and Alabama, respectively. It was a great photo opportunity, as pairing the two political positions against one another in a tossing duel appeared to be a welcomed event tradition.

As it turned out, Mobile Commissioner Steve Nodine threw his mullet 80 feet, while Escambia County Commissioner Valentino hurled his some 88 feet, making the State of Florida the clear-cut winner in the Commissioners' Mullet Toss Duel.

Steve Nodine, however, in a mere matter of days, proved to have much bigger problems than anyone ever expected.

***

The 2011 Mullet Toss enjoyed much nicer weather than the event the year prior. I spent the entire weekend at the Flora-Bama and was able to soak up many of the enthralling sights and sounds associated with what is justifiably tabbed as the "Gulf Coast's Largest Beach Party." In short, it lived up to its lofty billing.

The weather on Saturday was clear and balmy, making for a perfect day for beach voyeurism. In the afternoon I walked the crowded beach behind the Flora-Bama dotted with large, SEC battle flags—mainly of LSU, Alabama, Auburn and Florida, and took in the impressive, youthful exuberance of it all.

There were several innovative party operations going on the beach that day, including *Igloo* coolers retrofitted with amplified sound, tailgating tents, and even gas-powered daiquiri machines that started like a lawnmower would—with a hand crank.

One of the more memorable manifestations was a group of Louisiana kids who built a huge apparatus that hoisted a keg with clear tubes emanating from it into the air. Once the metal-framed, simple machine was engaged, the 16-gallon keg was amazingly lifted into the air so that up to five people could grab the tubes and suck the suds streaming down them. That afternoon I saw the group go through three such kegs, meaning they and their thirsty, reveling friends funneled nearly 50 gallons of cold draft beer. In retrospect, the Mullet Toss is not for the faint of heart, but it certainly is scenic, as you are guaranteed to see a multitude of young hard bodies in itsy-bitsy string bikinis and ultra-tight Speedos.

The Mullet Toss is one of the best beach parties you could ever attend. If you think you've got serious beach party game, give it a try. You will not be disappointed. The beach area directly behind the Flora-Bama is always a spectacular scene for those who love a true beach party—replete with young, beautiful people, great vibes and unlimited amounts of cold adult beverages. If you're up for it, they always have fun there during the last full weekend in April.

Chapter Nine
The Nashville Connection

"The music business is a cruel and shallow money trench, a long plastic hallway where thieves and pimps run free, and good men die like dogs. There's also a negative side."

-Hunter Stockton Thompson

On the weekend of May 1st and 2nd 2010, torrential downpours in the Southeast flooded the Tennessee capital of Nashville, elevating the Cumberland River 13 feet above its flood stage, causing an estimated $1 billion in property damage, and killing more than 30 people, making it one of the more expensive natural disasters in American history.

The torrential rains closed interstate highways, displaced thousands from their homes, prompted evacuations of hotels and nursing homes and turned city streets and parking lots into raging rivers. The western two thirds of the State of Tennessee saw between six and 20 inches of rain on Saturday, May 1st, with raging flooding spreading to Kentucky on Sunday May 2, 2010. More rain fell in Nashville over that long weekend than has ever been recorded in the city's history.

Nevertheless, with the other disaster raging—the Gulf oil spill, the national media seemed to ignore the worsening plight of the Music City. The Nashville floods never gained much of a foothold in the national conversation because the narrative simply wasn't as compelling.

Since it continually needs to fill airwaves and the Internet with new content, the media can only trade on a story's novelty for a few hours. It is new angles, new characters, and new chapters that keep a news story alive for longer periods. The Nashville narrative wasn't compelling enough to break the normal news cycle, so the main stream media just continued to blather on about the BP gusher in the Gulf of Mexico.

Much like the oil spill debacle, the Nashville flood had a similar local effect on business and commerce. Regular music and entertainment tourism came to a screeching halt as a result of the destructive deluge. Retail and hotel receipts were non-existent, as everyone headed for higher, dryer ground.

Singer-songwriters and musicians who made a living on Nashville's popular music row were forced to vacate their beloved home and workplace. Many of them made their way to Perdido Key and the Flora-Bama, a place that for years has been considered a welcome reprieve and respite for wayward artists needing a break from the all-consuming country music scene. One such artist was Hope Cassity, an aspiring young singer/songwriter who couldn't find work in Nashville as a result of the flood.

In early May 2010, Joe asked me to accompany him to see Hope Cassity play at a local Orange Beach bar and café, Joey's North Shore Hula-Hula Tiki Bar & Grill, which regularly featured live music played by musicians who also played at the Flora-Bama down the road. Despite great efforts to maintain, Joey's bar eventually closed at the beginning of 2011, another unfortunate victim of the soured gulf coast economy.

Hope Cassity is one of those young, struggling singer-songwriters you can't help but like and support. Her heartfelt lyrics and melodic voice, along with her sweet, Southern charm, make her irresistible. Hope hails from the Northern Alabama city of Monroeville. Like countless others before her with a dream, she made her way to Nashville to find a working niche in the ultra-competitive, unforgiving country music hub.

Despite her obvious talents and work ethic, Hope told me that her art has been disappointingly tabbed as something "in between country and pop, and not really country" by the omniscient Nashville music gatekeepers. Despite the unfair criticisms, she continues to create music independently and to hope that one day more people will recognize and appreciate her beautiful music.

Miss Meaghan Owens was another singer/songwriter who eventually hit the Flora-Bama scene. Joe dragged me out of my camper one evening to hear her at another infamous picking party at the residence of a local Flora-Bama regular on Old River.

Meaghan is one of those rare artists who you can literally sit and listen to while she sings the phone book. Her dulcet voice and youthful enthusiasm is infectious. She is a fabulous talent who is thankful for the opportunities Joe has provided her and her musician friends like Chris Newbury, the enigmatic Darby Jones and the unforgiveable Buzz Kiefer.

I say unforgiveable only because Buzz left a pregnant cat in Joe's keeping that eventually brought him and Bo Roberts a litter of meowing kittens. Joe of course took loving care with each, ensuring that they made it off to good homes. He even brought in a couple of stray kittens he found at a local apartment complex and gave them to the mama cat to nurse. Amazingly, she nursed the two new kittens like they were part of her own litter. I think Joe still has a couple of these cats.

Meaghan spoke glowingly of Joe. "Joe Gilchrist is the Archangel of songwriters. I heard about Joe Gilchrist and his place the Flora-Bama and checked it out on the Internet. I heard about this compassionate man who loved songwriters, who understood and loved what we do. It sounded like a dream—but he and his place are real. Joe is compassionate. He is a real guy, a deep guy. He is a real person."

A Wisconsin native, Miss Meaghan explained that the Flora-Bama was and remains a welcome reprieve for her. "Going to the Flora-Bama down on Perdido Key is always a healing experience for me and I would imagine it is like that for many songwriters. Nashville's rock stars and politicians can descend on you like vultures. It happened to me and I had to get out of there. The Flora-Bama was the perfect place for me to go. Joe got me and my musician friends gigs. He got us a great place to stay at the River House. He fed us good, home-cooked food. I found out that the Flora-Bama dream is absolutely real!"

Meaghan, when not touring, works to promote her favorite philanthropy, Guitars for Vets (G4V – *guitars4vets.org*) which notably explores the healing power of music in the hands of American military heroes.

One thing I noticed early and often while following Joe around and meeting so many artists is that making a living wage as a musician is a difficult gig—even in a good beach economy. In that same vein, I realized that a failing economy is a most unlikely place for laughter and song, as most of the potential customers are worried about their waning sustenance, instead of entertainment needs.

The summer of 2010 was a terribly difficult economic time for all musicians and music aficionados, for that matter. Folks were more concerned about keeping or getting a paying job than they were about pursuing worldly pleasures regularly reserved for leisure or vacation time in Perdido Key.

***

Of the many great artists and music legends who have endeared themselves to the island community by playing the stages at the Flora-Bama and the Silver Moon, perhaps none has made such a lasting impression and forged so many vivid, fond memories as the late, great Mickey Newbury.

A prolific crooner and special man of words, Mickey Newbury was a consummate artist, years ahead of his time, and certainly one of the more proficient writers and players to grace The Line. Mickey left behind as many wonderful songs as he did good friends, a loving family and a special son, Chris, who inherited much of his father's remarkable writing and vocal talents; and was also blessed with his own. Chris is a regular player at the Silver Moon today. We will talk more about him later, after we talk about his amazing father.

A Houston, Texas native, Mickey Newbury (1940-2002) was among the most influential American songwriters of the twentieth century. As a teenager Newbury locked himself in his room for hours, writing poetry and picking the guitar. Before he went off to the service in England as a 19-year old Air Force enrollee, he even formed a band, a doo-wop group called The Embers. After three years of military service in England, Mickey returned to the states where he continued his visceral songwriting pursuit.

Back in the States in 1962, just before the original Flora-Bama was being born and subsequently razed, Mickey reportedly lived out of a 1954 Pontiac and traveled around the Southern states of Texas, Tennessee, and Louisiana looking for and playing gigs and working as an extra hand on shrimp boats—anything he could do to stay alive. He predictably landed in Nashville, and in 1964, signed a publishing contract with Acuff-Rose. He moved to Nashville in 1965, and at about this time, his first child, Joe, was born. Shortly thereafter, Jimmy Elledge was the first artist to cover a Mickey Newbury song, "Just as Long as that Someone is You."

Mickey Newbury's breakout year was 1966. The music industry took notice. Don Gibson hit the Country Top Ten with Newbury's "Funny Familiar Forgotten Feelings" and Tom Jones scored a universal smash hit with the same song. In 1968, Mickey amazingly saw three number one songs along with a number five, on four different music charts; "Just Dropped In" (To See What Condition My Condition Was In) on the Pop/Rock chart by the First Edition, "Sweet Memories" on Easy Listening by Andy Williams, "Time is a Thief" on the R&B chart by Solomon Burke, and "Here Comes the Rain Baby" on the

Country chart by Eddy Arnold. No other artist has replicated this astounding feat. That same year, Mickey's first album, Harlequin Melodies, was released by RCA.

Mickey met New Christy Minstrel member Susan Pack while on a blind date in 1967. Although he did not see her again for two years, they were married soon after nonetheless, and lived on a houseboat on Old Hickory Lake on the outskirts of Nashville. From 1967 to 1971, Mickey released a trilogy of blockbuster albums. Produced at the garage-turned Cinderella Studios outside of Nashville, Tennessee, "Looks Like Rain," "Frisco Mabel Joy" and "Heaven Help The Child," are all still considered bona fide masterpieces.

Mickey was one of the most creative and influential minds in Nashville. It was Newbury who convinced Roger Miller to record Kris Kristofferson's "Me & Bobby McGee," which went on to catapult Kristofferson into the endearing limelight as country music's top songwriter.

Mickey was certainly one of the original outlaws of the 1970's and 1980's Outlaw Country Movement. Ralph Emery called him "The first hippie-cowboy," and along with Johnny Cash and Roger Miller, he was one of the first to eschew the rigid conventions of the Nashville music scene. After being disappointed by the production methods used by Felton Jarvis on his debut album, Newbury secured a release from his contract with RCA and signed the first offer he received complying with his stipulation that he could either produce his own albums, or choose the producer.

Newbury was also responsible for getting Townes Van Zandt and Guy Clark to move to Nashville and pursue careers as songwriters. However, unlike some, he had no desire to cash-in on the Outlaw movement.

Following the birth of their first child, Chris, in 1973, Mickey and Susan moved to Oregon, to Susan's hometown, to raise the children, as a daughter, Leah, followed in 1977. In 1980, Mickey, at the age of 40, was the youngest songwriter ever inducted into the *Nashville Songwriter's Hall of Fame*.

Mickey recorded several albums throughout the 1970's for Elektra and ABC/Hickory Records, all of them critically praised, albeit financially unsuccessful. In the 1980's, after achieving early songwriting fame and acclaim, Mickey sought a reprieve from music to concentrate on his growing family and his golf game. Another son, Stephen, arrived in 1983, and another daughter, Laura Shane, followed in 1986.

In the early 1990's, Mickey started writing, recording, and performing again, urged by friends Bob Rosemurgy, Marty Hall, and Owsley Mannier. In 1995, Mickey's health began to suffer, but he continued to create wonderful music. From 1995 to 2002 he was busy, almost doubling his album count. He also focused on other creative endeavors, beginning work on children's books based on his songs that told stories. On September 29, 2002, at the age of 62, Mickey Newbury lost his long battle with lung disease (pulmonary fibrosis) and passed away in his sleep, at home in Springfield, Oregon.

Mickey Newbury's love was the music, not the business. Among his songwriting and musical peers, he was always seen as a champion of the songwriter. Among his family members and associates, he was known as a wonderful son, husband, father, and friend.

Mickey's most popular (and most often covered) song is "American Trilogy," one he arranged, but was made universally popular by Elvis Presley, who included it as part of his regular concert routine in the 1970's, thereby making it a veritable showstopper. It is a medley of three different 19th century songs—"Dixie," a blackface minstrel tune that became the unofficial anthem of the Confederacy since the Civil War; "All My Trials," originally a Bahamian lullaby, but closely related to African American spirituals, and well-known through folk music revivalists; and "The Battle Hymn of the Republic," the marching song of the Union Army during the United States Civil War.

Although he considered himself a songwriter first and singer second, Mickey's albums are loved worldwide equally as much as his wonderful songs. Newbury offered the following choice advice to writers, "Write what you are or you'll become what you write."

Many consider Mickey Newbury to be the best of the best. Kris Kristofferson says, "God, I learned more about songwriting from Mickey than I did any other single human being. To me he was a songbird. He comes out with amazing words and music... I'm sure that I never would have written "Bobby McGee," and "Sunday Morning Coming Down" if I had never known Mickey. He was my hero and still is."

Mickey Newburry amazingly penned songs that were recorded by more than 1,100 different artists, including Elvis Presley, Johnny Cash, Roy Orbison and other major American music stars. He also produced an impressive 35 albums.

Mickey Newbury was much like a singing poet. The song lyrics he produced were in most cases pure poetry artfully set to well-arranged music. His style was as deliberate as it was meaningful, and in many ways as an artist he was ahead of his time and industry peers. Further, as a songwriter he had few equals.

"They'd all shut up and listen to Mickey. He was just too good. He had no equal. That was his only problem," said Ken Lambert.

"Mickey was so full of love. He made you feel it," stated Jay Hawkins.

"A sweet memory…is what Mickey Newberry is," added New Jersey native Rick Whaley, a regular player and singer with Lee Anne Creswell at the Bama and the Silver Moon.

American music legend Johnny Cash once aptly introduced Mickey Newbury before he played a televised concert. "I respect the difficulty of crafting a line that expresses a single heartfelt thought, and this man does it so well."

Noted superstar singer/songwriter Kris Kristofferson said of Newbury, "Mickey deliberately defies labels. He is neither country nor soul…behind the deceptive simplicity of some of his lyrics, there are levels of mental landscape that can take you in some strange directions, past the edges of understanding."

"Mickey said so much with so few words. He was unlike any other. He is greatly missed," said Joe Gilchrist.

***

There are so many artists who have graced the stages at the Flora-Bama and the Silver Moon, it would be nearly impossible to note all of them in this book. However, there are some that must be mentioned, as their noted presence on The Line has helped foster the institution's glowing legend as a premier venue for live music.

One such artist was Larry Jon Wilson.

Joe called me in the spring of 2010, to hear a concert at the Silver Moon that included his long-time friend, Larry Jon Wilson and rare auto harpist/guitarist/singer, Gove Scrivenor. Scrivenor's talent is another gift well worth mentioning, as he is the only person I have ever known to play the unusually rare and equally beautiful, auto harp. A long-time favorite of the Flora-Bama regulars, Gove has played on many big stages, including the world-famous Austin City Limits and with the now-departed June Carter and Mother Maybelle Carter, who also knew well the auto harp's mysterious, melodic wonders.

Swainsboro, Georgia native Larry Jon Wilson was one of the same noted musicians from the renowned "Outlaw Music Genre" already mentioned. During his noteworthy singing and songwriting career he recorded "Through the Eyes of Little Children" and "I Betcha Heaven's on a Dirt Road," among other popular songs.

A polymer chemist by education and trade, Larry Jon Wilson began penning songs somewhat late in life, after his thirtieth birthday. He mourned the passing of his father, learned his wife was pregnant and welcomed the gift of a Martin guitar all within a 24-hour period, prompting him to embrace a later life of music. Larry Jon developed a songwriting style that reflected his bucolic Georgia upbringing.

Joe introduced me to Larry Jon, who appeared to have seen better days. I was told that he was having severe health problems. Based on accounts from Joe and others who knew him well, Larry Jon was a much huskier and healthier fellow during his younger years, when he was raising hell like the other outlaws musical innovators of his day. A picture of Larry Jon that hung in the Silver Moon for years depicted the likeness of a broad-necked crooner one would think twice of ever tumbling with.

In an article on Larry Jon's passing by Peter Cooper of the *Tennessean*, Larry Jon was quoted, "Some people have used the 'Outlaw' tag effectively for a career move, but I don't think 'career move' has ever entered my thinking. When I was in Nashville, we did the streets an awful long time, and we weren't exactly holding prayer meetings. I loved my drinking days. I stopped in the 1980's, but they were good. I'm not ashamed of any of it."

I sat and talked to a feeble Larry Jon for a while that afternoon at the Silver Moon before his evening performance, which proved to be his last on this earth. Larry Jon died less than four months later on June 21, 2010, from stroke complications. I remember him as a consummate Southern gentleman and songwriter/poet who happened to also be a great performer. Many who met or knew Larry Jon and his music share the same sentiment.

Like so many other devout artists of his time, Larry Jon never recorded a huge hit that made him famous or that brought him great wealth. Despite many accolades and an adoring fan base, he never found the kind of wealth or fame he rightly deserved as an artist.

In 1980, at 40, he left the music industry, only to return a few years later at the Frank Brown Songwriter's Festival in Perdido Key, Florida. After that event he began touring again, and accepted invitations to play as late as 2003.

If you have ever seen the documentary on the Flora-Bama titled, "The Last Great American Roadhouse," it is Larry Jon's flannel-warm, baritone voice that cheerfully narrates it. According to Joe, Larry Jon loved coming to the Perdido Key area to relax and enjoy life with friends and to write songs.

In 2009, the Larry Jon Wilson album, his first in 29 years, made many fans and critics re-examine his ability and impact on the songwriting world. He toured the United Kingdom briefly before his health failed, re-introducing to many youngsters like me the forgotten novelty of the singer-songwriter. Larry Jon signed a copy of this final album for me, and the poetic creation bearing his signature is one of my favorites. He is likely now reciting his soothing work to angels.

Another former, notable songwriter friend of the Flora-Bama was Hank Cochran. Like so many other consummate songwriters, Cochran enjoyed the sights and sounds on The Line as much as anyone. In fact, before his health failed him, Cochran was seen just a few weeks earlier at the Silver Moon, enjoying the regular music lineup. A Mississippi native, Cochran was known for his emotional songs, "I Fall to Pieces" and "She's Got You," both recorded by artist Patsy Cline in the early 1960's.

In 1960, Cochran was reportedly on a date inside a movie theatre when the film he was watching inspired him to words. After the feature he immediately exited the movie theatre and headed home. Fifteen minutes later he had already composed "Make the World Go Away," which was cut first by Ray Price and then later by Eddy Arnold, with both enjoying signature hits with the song. Cochran later wrote "Ocean Front Property" for George Strait and "Don't You Ever Get Tired (of Hurting Me)," for Ronnie Milsap.

Cochran wrote several successful songs for Burl Ives and while he was writing songs for Pamper Music and moonlighting as a performer in Nashville's Tootsie's Orchid Lounge, he encouraged Pamper Music's management to sign a talented young songwriter, Willie Nelson.

In 2008, Hank allowed longtime Flora-Bama performer Lee Anne Creswell to come to his home and select an album of uncut songs he wrote, which she later released as "Lee Anne Sings Hank Cochran." Cochran passed away July 15, 2010, at the age of 74.

Another gone but not forgotten songwriting friend of the Flora-Bama was Larry Butler, a Pensacola native, who passed away January 20, 2012, at the age of 69.

Butler was the only person in Nashville history to win an All-Genre Producer of the Year Grammy. Butler wrote and produced songs for Johnny Cash, Charlie Rich, John Denver, Bill Anderson, Dottie West and Waylon Jennings, among others. However, his biggest impact as a songwriter was in penning and producing material for Kenny Rogers. Butler helped Rogers smoothly transition from rock to country with hits like "The Gambler," "Lucille," and "Coward of the County." The Gambler album, since 1978, has sold an unbelievable 36 million copies.

According to Joe, Larry Butler was in Hollywood in 1976 for the Grammy Awards. That was the year he won for best country song with "(Hey Won't You Play) Another Somebody Done Somebody Wrong Song" by B.J. Thomas. Well, after the Grammy Awards ceremony was over, Butler found himself at a party, enjoying cocktails with James Cagney and Jimmy Stewart. There was a piano nearby and Cagney and Stewart talked Butler into playing his winning song, "(Hey Won't You Play)," and they all three sung it together.

Butler collaborated with many other famous artists, and was a prolific writer of hit songs, like "Hard to be Humble" for Mac Davis and "Are You on the Road to Loving Me Again," for Debbie Boone.

Butler at one time headed a publishing company that signed talented writers, including Mickey Newbury and Dean Dillon. Songs written by his company were recorded by George Strait, Keith Whitley and Vern Gosdin, among others. Like so many other famous songwriting friends, Butler is gone from the Flora-Bama, but not forgotten for the artful contributions he has made to the creative community that faithfully supports it.

***

America songwriting legend Billy Joe Shaver is another noteworthy friend and favored former player at the Flora-Bama. Once quoted as saying, "Simple don't need greasing," he has been aptly depicted as a roughneck scribe.

Shaver is as renowned as a songwriter as he is a true outlaw country legend. A wizard with basic words and phrasing, he possesses a simplistic, metaphorical style that artfully invokes the heart and mind. Shaver knows well the power of fewer words, allowing his listeners, through their own unique life perspectives, to fill in the blanks. Shaver is also a supreme survivor, as his life has been one not without great hardship. "I wrote most of my songs to get in the house, get back in the house, or to stay alive," he once said.

Hailing from Corsicana, Texas, Shaver was raised during the 1940's by his mother, aunt and grandmother after his father abandoned them. As a result of his difficult family situation, Shaver often spent time with his aunt, who preferred dating black men.

In his book, "Honky Tonk Hero," published by the *University of Texas Press*, Shaver related the story of how one day as a youngster while he was in the care of his aunt, she left him with one of her friends, who happened to be a black woman. Shaver explained how this woman of color brought him into the segregated bathroom stall at a local department store so she could use the facilities. He further explained, in vivid detail, how she pulled up her skirt, revealing the sacred area between her legs, which he described as "a crow with a red ribbon in its mouth."

As a boy Shaver occasionally went to work with his mother at her job in a local nightclub, and that exposed him early to country music. Shaver chose not to attend school after junior high to help his uncle pick cotton. However, he admitted he occasionally went back to school to play sports.

After joining the Navy at 17, and upon discharge, he worked a number of dead end jobs, including an attempt at being a rodeo cowboy. He then met Brenda Joyce Tindell, married her and had a son, John Edwin, who was known simply as "Eddy." The couple divorced and remarried several times.

Shaver once took a job at a lumber mill. One day while on the job, his writing hand, his right—got caught in the sawing mechanism, and he lost most of his index and middle fingers as a result of the painful accident. An infection set in but he eventually healed and taught himself to play the guitar, despite the modest handicap.

Shaver quickly came to the firm realization that life is too short to do something you don't enjoy. He embarked on a hitchhiking trip to Los Angeles. Instead, his free ride delivered him to Nashville, Tennessee, where he found a job as a songwriter for $50 per week. His writing quickly gained the attention of Waylon Jennings, who used his songs to mostly comprise his popular album, "Honky Tonk Heroes." Other notable entertainers like Elvis Presley and Kris Kristofferson soon started recording his songs. This acclaim eventually led to a record deal.

Like many struggling singer-songwriting types, Shaver did not immediately find financial success. The recording companies he initially contracted with soon failed. Although he has never gained universal recognition as a singer, he has collaborated with some of the greatest rock and country artists of his time, like Willie Nelson, Nanci Griffith, Chuck Leavell, the Allman Brothers' Dickey Betts, Charlie Daniels, Flaco Jimenez and Al Kooper, to name just a few.

In 1996, Billy Joe had a part in the movie *The Apostle*, appearing opposite his friend, Robert Duvall. He also had additional parts in another Duvall film made in 2003, *Secondhand Lions*, and in *The Wendell Baker Story* in 2005.

After he lost both his wife and mother to cancer in 1999, Billy Joe lost his son and longtime guitarist, Eddy, at the young age of 38, from a heroin overdose. The following year he almost followed them into eternity when he experienced cardiac arrest on stage while performing an Independence Day concert at Guene Hall in New Braunsfels, Texas. In 2002, after a successful heart procedure, he returned to the stage to release the album "Freedom's Child."

In March 2007, in Lorena, Texas, about ten miles south of Waco, Shaver was involved in a fracas outside Papa Joe's Texas Saloon. In that imbroglio he was accused of shooting a man by the name of Billy Bryant Coker in the face with a handgun. Witnesses reported that Shaver, prior to shooting, asked the alleged victim, "Where do you want it?" and that after shots were fired, he said, "Tell me you are sorry" and "No one tells me to shut up."

Coker contended the attack was unprovoked. Shaver's attorney argued his client shot in self defense after Coker threatened Billy Joe with a knife. Three years later, in April 2010, Shaver was acquitted after testifying he acted in self defense.

Shaver has served as the spiritual advisor to Texas independent gubernatorial candidate, Kinky Friedman. He is a recipient of the Americana Music Convention's Lifetime Achievement Award in songwriting. He lives in Waco, Texas.

Billy Joe was the featured act at the 2011 Frank Brown Songwriter's Festival. He charmed everyone that fantastic week when he performed multiple times for many thankful fans. In addition to performing at the Silver Moon to an intimate few, he performed on both stages at the Flora-Bama—inside and outside, making for a most memorable FBSF, pumping out "I'm Just an Old Chunk of Coal," "Been That way Since the Get-Go" and "Whacko From Waco," among others.

***

Like he was with Mickey Newbury, Joe is friends today with Chris Newbury, Mickey's son. Chris and Bo Roberts, another singer/songwriter and all-around character who has undoubtedly helped make the Flora-Bama entertainment community what it is today, lived together when I met them in the spring of 2010, in a ranch home property owned by Joe near the Naval Aviation Museum off Blue Angel Parkway, in West Pensacola, Florida, about thirty minutes from the Flora-Bama down the Gulf Beach Highway. It was a place Joe would eventually have to move into, due to his bankruptcy.

The living room in the old ranch home off of Blue Angel and South Loop was turned into a recording studio by Bo and Chris. Bo Roberts is an experienced songwriter and him teaming up with Chris—a guy who was weaned on music made by his award-winning, legendary father, Mickey, was an interesting match.

The two enjoyed listening to the created wonders of deceased Texas folk legend/songwriter Townes Van Zant, trying to glean something not yet fully understood about his unlikely genius. Van Zant, a Forth Worth, Texas native, struggled with addiction most of his life, but still managed to move many with his art, through penned songs like "To live is to fly," "No place to fall" and "If I needed you." Van Zant succumbed to complications of a life hard-lived in 2007, in Mount Juliet, Tennessee. He was 52 years old.

Chris Newbury is as soft-spoken as he is friendly. I am certain it must be difficult following in the heavy footsteps of a songwriting virtuoso, but Chris handles it pretty well. In the short time I've known Chris he has grown considerably as an artist. He continues to improve on his singing poet style that he obviously inherited. Much like his father, Chris communicates as much as he entertains while singing, as much in word as in heartfelt expression. During much of 2010, and 2011, Chris and Bo were a popular singer/songwriter duo featured at the Silver Moon on Thursday nights. They became a favorite of the many regulars and tourists just passing through the area. On one night they performed I brought my girls, Madilyn Amelia, 11, and Emma Claire, 9, to hear them play and sing. The girls loved them, as they replayed again and again on their smart phones the video recordings of the songs Bo and Chris sang to them that evening. We also later had fun talking about the meanings of the songs Bo and Chris sang, and how we each had slightly different perceptions.

One of the important pieces of the Flora-Bama puzzle that few know about is Mike Locklin. Mike is the sound guy at the Flora-Bama. He is also a pretty good guitar player, so he has a keen ear and a working expertise in sound systems. Mike makes everything run smoothly for all the musicians and their musical equipment, and he of course always ensures quality sound, which is the lofty standard he always maintains.

***

In the summer of 2010, Joe was still living in a modest, elevated, two-bedroom home on Old River about two and a half miles east from the Flora-Bama, that he purchased in the mid 1990's. The place was great. It had a swimming pool and a hot tub out back and was a popular hangout for many of the musicians who would often come over for what Joe and the other local characters called "guitar pulls."

A guitar pull, or "picking party," was and still is a party that Joe had (and still does have) at his house where musicians share a guitar, passing it amongst themselves while taking turns singing their favorite songs. These guitar pulls are always great fun. One such picking party that summer was particularly memorable.

Joe called me one early weekend afternoon and informed me that he was having another of his noted guitar pulls at his house on Old River. He told me to grab something to contribute to the feast and something to drink and to come over to his place in the early evening.

Per his request I grabbed some fish filets and a six pack of cold bottled beer at the fresh seafood market located underneath the Theo Barrs Bridge spanning the Intracoastal Canal, and headed to Joe's. When I got there the place was already buzzing with activity. There were several people cooking in the kitchen—frying fish and preparing many other delectable Southern fixings. There was potato salad, tossed salad, various fresh breads and even dessert.

When I arrived I was introduced by Joe to a woman he simply called "Beverly Jo." She was barefoot, in blue jean cut-off shorts and a plain white tee shirt, and was sweating profusely from the heat emanating from the pot-cluttered, open stovetop and the broiling summer time sun outside; as the door leading to the pool deck was constantly opening and closing. Beverly Jo wiped her unoccupied hand on her shorts and offered it. I shook it, exchanged pleasantries, gave her a smile and continued meeting and greeting the many other musicians and regulars in attendance.

Later that evening, after everyone had eaten, and the dishes were for the most part done, we all settled down in Joe's austere living room and began another anticipated guitar pull. Bo Roberts started things off. Rick Whaley followed him. As the guitar made its way around to me, a non-musician, I politely handed it to Beverly Jo, who was seated to my right, awkwardly sideways, in a padded rocking chair. She seemed indifferent to everything going on around her, and not the least bit concerned about having to play guitar and sing.

I did not know Beverly Jo. I had never met her. I had no idea she was an accomplished musician; as by look, word and deed that afternoon she had not at all given me that impression. She received the guitar and began to gingerly strum its strings. Expressionless, she implored to everyone, asking them what she should play. I remember thinking to myself as she did this, in a gentle monotone, that she didn't really look or sound like a singer or a songwriter, and that she might even struggle with the task of playing for a smattering of Joe's legitimate, accomplished, song-writing friends. Never in my life was I more wrong. The old adage was, in this case, certainly true. Never judge a book by its cover—or a singer/songwriter by their looks.

Someone there asked Beverly Jo to play "the song she had been working on earlier that day." She agreed and began playing and singing in a way that immediately evoked emotion. Beverly Jo, in particular, was Beverly Jo Scott, a Mobile native whose star had blossomed and taken her across the pond to Europe—mainly Belgium and France, where she became, and to this day, remains, a bona fide rock star with a most faithful following. She lives most of the time in Europe, and only occasionally returns home to Alabama. As it turned out, I was extremely lucky to be there that evening.

About five seconds into her piece the hair on my arms stood straight. Goose bumps quickly followed, riddling the surface of my skin on both arms. She sounded like an angel, sent straight from heaven. She was fantastic, and when she was done, I selfishly didn't want her to pass the guitar to the musicians who had preceded her. I also remember, while she sang, glancing over toward the direction of Bo Roberts. Bo's face bore the incredulous countenance of a child who had just witnessed a small miracle. Beverly Jo was nothing short of amazing.

Later that evening Beverly Jo treated us again when she sang her rendition of "Old Alabam'," and it again brought chills. It was then that I realized a little more of the musical "magic" that Joe often talked about. During her "Old

Alabam'" performance Joe and I made eye contact. He just smiled proudly, knowing well that I was blown away by her performance.

    I will never forget hearing and watching the supremely talented Beverly Jo Scott move us with her words put to music that evening. Moving forward, I was different; and certainly better off having experienced it; and that's the always beautiful, equally unexplainable, power of art.

Chapter Ten

Music to the Rescue

"I said as I sat by the edge of the sea,
A music-hall show would look bully to me;
I thought as I walked by the edge of the dunes,
Why should the Devil have all the good tunes?"

-*Frederick Lewis Allen*

By the middle of May 2010, things were really going badly for the beleaguered gulf coast. As a result of the failing economy and the billowing uncapped BP oil well, beach tourism slowed to a mere crawl—a fraction of what entrepreneurs needed to make payroll. With their hopes of a profitable summer tourist season effectively dashed, many area residents had fallen into a most unshakeable funk, as they faced the harrowing prospect of losing both their businesses and their livelihoods.

However, during the weekend of May 14-16, 2010, the inaugural Hangout Music Festival began, bringing to the beach in Gulf Shores, Alabama a bevy of some of the world's most talented musical artists. The unprecedented, three-day outdoor concert event showcased the following Friday artists: The Zac Brown Band, The Black Crowes, the North Mississippi All-Stars, Orianthi, Allison Krauss, Robert Randolph, Brett Dennen, Davy Knowles, Girl Talk, Pnuma Trio, Jeff Austin & Friends, Kirsten Price, Papa Mali & Friends, Rachel Goodrich, El Cantador, Ben Arthur and Hightide Blues, among others.

Saturday at the beach brought John Legend, Government Mule (Warren Haynes), the Funky Meters, Ozomatli, The Roots, Rodrigo Y Gabriela, Grace Potter and the Nocturnals, Jerry Jeff Walker, Jakob Dylan & Three Legs, The Whigs, Toubab Krewe, A.A. Bondy, Moon Taxi, Wild Sweet Orange, Honey Island Swamp Band, Rustlanders and Jon Black.

Sunday showcased Trey Anastasio & Tab, Ben Harper & Relentless7, Michael Franti & Spearhead, Keller Williams, Ray LaMontagne, Guster, Matisyahu, Blind Boys of Alabama, Need to Breathe, OK GO, Black Joe Lewis & the Honeybears, Alo, Matt Hires, Kristy Lee, Roman Street, Rollin' in the Hay and The Cary Lane Band.

I have many fond memories of that entertaining weekend. The multi-day concert was well-attended by concert aficionados from all over the Deep South and abroad, and the music was outstanding, as I listened to several bands that I had no idea existed.

I can remember vividly on Sunday being called to the stage where Guster was playing and singing "Satellite," which I thought was a fantastic tune. I remember firmly shaking hands with Michael Franti, of Spearhead, telling him that I dug his art. He was more than gracious with the crowd, taking cell phone pictures with everyone who wanted a souvenir shot with him.

I recall on Saturday the many unique percussion rhythms of Toubaob Krewe, the brother and sister Spanish guitar duo of Rodrigo and Gabriela aptly covering Metallica songs, Warren Haynes making his guitar gently weep and old-time outlaw Jerry Jeff Walker singing about wanting "to go home with the armadillo."

Friday was another memorable day as the Zac Brown Band and the Black Crowes were consecutive showstoppers against a pastel sunset backdrop. There were many impressive, indelible performances that weekend.

A few of the artists predictably used their time on stage to openly voice their bitter discontent with British Petroleum for fouling up the gulf beaches and the normally lucrative summer tourist season.

Ben Harper, a Claremont, California-based singer and songwriter, used an assortment of expletives to communicate his BP-laden invective, much to the crowd's raucous approval. This was a concert that was formally dedicated to the gulf coast comeback, and Harper obviously wanted to ensure his own attempt at affecting consumer payback. He urged the crowd to never again buy BP gasoline. The crowd roared and clapped in fiery affirmation. To this day I think of Ben Harper's blistering appeal whenever I look for a gas station to fill my thinning tank.

In addition to serving as a catharsis for the catastrophe survivors and a rallying cry for the impending full economic recovery, the three-day concert was a huge financial boon to the area, as it brought tens of thousands of concertgoers who rented condos and hotel rooms and ate and drank in the many beach restaurants and bars from Gulf Shores to Orange Beach—despite the looming threat of oil. Even the Flora-Bama, a few miles down the road from the concert locale of Gulf Shores, saw a healthy increase in patrons.

The well-planned concert event was also a quintessential demonstration of the healing power of music against a beautiful backdrop of gleaming turquoise and silver sand. Many times during the concert I took notice of how gorgeous the scene was. The early evening concerts were particularly scenic, as the sun dipped slowly into the western sky behind the stage facing east, creating a kaleidoscope of soft-hued colors to complement the soothing opal glow of the Gulf of Mexico.

Joe and I attended the Saturday beachside events together. The consummate promoter, Joe insisted that we distribute to passersby hand leaflets bearing the daily Flora-Bama music schedule; and in doing so we ran into several interesting characters.

One of them was Mike Becker of the popular concert retailer, *Blues Conspiracy*. Mike, who lives on nearby Innerarity Point, is a traveling salesman of authentic rock n' roll and blues apparel. With his wife and mobile store—a large, customized vending truck, he frequents bigger outdoor events and concerts like the Hangout Festival all over the country, selling licensed merchandise of the Grateful Dead, Bob Marley, Jimi Hendrix, Peter Tosh, Incubus, the Red Hot Chili Peppers and many other well-known, iconic artists.

Mike is another interesting character. An accomplished picker and singer in his own right, over twenty years ago he told me he was released from prison and needed a job. He landed at The Line and Joe told him that if he was so inclined he could wash dishes in the kitchen at the Flora-Bama. Mike said he took the opportunity—because it was a job—and he often credits Joe with saving him, as he really needed a paycheck at the time.

Mike eventually moved on with his business idea for *Blues Conspiracy*, (Bluesconspiracy.com) but before he did in 2004, after Hurricane Ivan, he helped Joe and Pat set up the popular tee shirt trailer in front of the Flora-Bama near the edge of the beach highway, allowing them to affect a much larger marketing presence. Today the inauspicious trailer remains a huge income generator, selling Flora-Bama tee shirts, hats, worthwhile books, CD's for the artists who play at the Flora-Bama, and other fun souvenir and novelty items bearing the Flora-Bama's fun-filled likeness.

Another character we bumped into that day was Susie Ragsdale, a fabulous singer songwriter whose father is the popular 1960's and 1970's television entertainer, Ray Stevens. Susie now lives mainly in Nashville, Tennessee, but she comes home often to visit her mom, who still lives in the area.

Joe was ecstatic to see Susie. He asked her to come back down to play a special concert at the Silver Moon, which she did a few weeks later. She finished that concert by playing her father's 1970 Grammy-winning song for best contemporary vocal, "Everything is Beautiful (In its own way)." It was a wonderful song that completed an equally great concert. As a side note, on the original version of the song, Susie and her sister sang backup for their daddy—along with an entire second grade class from Oak Hill Elementary School in Nashville, Tennessee. The song began with the children's chorus singing the opening lines of a popular Bible school hymn, "Jesus Loves the Little Children."

In the days after the three-day event, the Hangout Concert received rave media and patron reviews. It was then announced that Fairhope native Jimmy Buffet and a few of his musician friends planned to put on their own beach concert—free of charge—at the same spot (The Hangout at the end of Interstate 59 in Gulf Shores) in July to help the area beset with so many difficulties. Buffet hit the airwaves, newspapers and social media to explain the plan that 30,000 free tickets would be made available online for the taking. However, due to the incredible Internet demand for the free tickets, accommodation availability quickly evaporated, along with the 30,000 complimentary tickets—in reportedly less than an hour.

Predictably, many of the former free tickets showed up on E-Bay for sale at a hefty price. Furthermore, it was also revealed that many of the Gulf Shores and Orange Beach high-rise condominium developments received large chunks of tickets to package with their concert weekend lodging and resort offerings. The resulting angry outcry from local rank and file Parrotheads was loud; and they quickly got notice from Chief Jimmy.

Buffet recognized that many had trouble getting the free tickets and subsequently worked with organizers to get even more complimentary tickets issued for the unprecedented open, beach concert. To his credit, it worked, as it seemed by the time the concert date finally arrived, that tickets were no longer an issue. In total, it was reported that over 35,000 free concert tickets were issued for the event. Attendance, and the resulting interest in the rare benefit concert, was fantastic.

Jimmy Buffet, who was born on Christmas Day just like Kenny Stabler, has been a friend and admirer of the Flora-Bama for many years. Since he has found international fame and stardom sharing his unique, island approach to living and enjoying life, he has maintained his obvious affinity for The Line by singing several songs about it, like the popular number, "Bama Breeze."

I went to the free Jimmy Buffet beach concert in Gulf Shores with Joe and a few other regulars. Before we went down to *The Hangout* we painted a large banner on an old sheet to hold up, and then later hang in the crowd, that read, "Flora-Bama Loves Jimmy Buffet." Joe greatly appreciated Jimmy's effort to help the area, and furthermore, he is and has been a fan of Jimmy Buffet and his music for some time.

Joe said he remembers Jimmy coming to the Flora-Bama fairly often and Joe is grateful for the many times Jimmy has acknowledged the area when he is on stage performing. "Jimmy Buffett has always been kind to the Flora-Bama, and he's always kind to the Gulf Coast. We just went up there to show support and respect for Jimmy Buffett, as he does something to represent our area."

Joe also recalled a trip to New York City in September 2007, to see Buffet play in Madison Square Garden when Jimmy, while he was playing on stage, mentioned and recognized Joe among the throng and mentioned his iconic Flora-Bama Lounge on the Alabama and Florida state line.

The 2010 Jimmy Buffet Gulf Coast Benefit concert went off without a hitch. It was both amazing and equally wonderful that so many people from across the South and the United States could and would work together to help the area challenged by the egregious environmental and economic setback. Like many other things that Jimmy touches, the free concert, which was televised live on Country Music Television and later re-aired on the same network, turned out to be a huge success, bringing thousands of music loving tourists to the beaches. These were people who otherwise would have never come to the area, as it was erroneously thought, thanks to the main stream media, that the Gulf Shores beaches were covered completely in muddy, dark brown oil, even though everyone that lived and played there knew otherwise.

At least for a weekend, anyhow, things were better. Merchants made much -needed money and more importantly—many people from out of state witnessed and realized first-hand that the media had been wholly misleading— that the area's gorgeous white sand beaches were not ruined by BP's spilled oil.

These revelers saw that the Gulf Shores, Orange Beach and Perdido Key areas were still a ripe vacation destination, with its magnetic draw—its pristine beaches—still firmly intact. But alas, the power of perception had mightily formed.

The reality was that the 2010 summer tourist season, because of the ignorance of BP, the callousness of the media and the ineptitude of the government—was effectively shot to hell. It was an unavoidable loss in many ways for coastal dwellers. In comparison to sales during prior good economic years, it was a small portion of the regular expected take. Further, the business horizon was tarnished with the din of an unprecedented economic uncertainty, as the United States government seemed bent on only printing more money for misguided stimulus and bailout projects that fattened the wallets of Washington insiders, campaign donors and fat cat bank executives, while the rank and file American suffered.

Public confidence in the federal government among Southerners was an oxymoron. In the Redneck Riviera, a place that for years had made its keeping on principally the success of others able to afford a beach vacation, it seemed that no one was spared by the calamity of the multiple tragedies.

The BP Oil Spill, President Barack Hussein Obama's debilitating, stimulus package and bailout-guided great recession were all money killers to the common man. Further, a restrictive business environment spawned by the passage of Federal Health Care legislation against the backdrop of free-falling real estate and stock markets depleted the personal wealth statements and financial confidence of anyone in the proverbial money game.

***

After the July 4, 2010 holiday weekend I stopped by Joe's house on what proved to be a difficult Monday evening. I found Joe in a particularly somber mood. He looked worn out, as if he had nothing left in his tank. He was not his regular, animated self. I could tell something was terribly wrong; that something was really bothering him, as by dress and countenance he gave every awkward appearance. Of course, in hindsight, at that time, I sometimes forgot that he had actually lost nearly $40 million as a result of over-speculating during the recent government-caused real estate bubble. It tortured him; as it rightly would most people who had lost so much.

The U.S. Government enacted multiple policies that adversely affected the markets. The Jimmy Carter and Bill Clinton administrations made home ownership a right by forcing banks, through the Community Reinvestment Act (CRA) and its subsequent amendments, to make bad loans to people who had no business owning a home. They had no business owning a home because their ability to pay their hefty monthly mortgage for that home was non-existent. Of course, the majority of these toxic loans ultimately ended in foreclosure, prompting a massive housing market glut and the imminent bursting of the over-inflated housing bubble.

"I don't think it makes any sense for anyone to want to be an entrepreneur in America anymore," Joe commented, much to my utter shock and dismay.

It was such a chilling, near-blasphemous statement. Joe was one of the most successful entrepreneurs I had ever known—a true innovator and risk taker. Somebody who had created something special out of what was formerly nothing, employing many and bringing prosperity to an entire gulf coast community in the process. The specter of financial defeat loomed large as we sat on his screened in porch overlooking Old River on an otherwise overcast, humid summer evening.

He continued, "There is too much government. It has become too expensive. Our government is one that requires too much of its citizens. The current government is a disincentive to innovate, to put forth new ideas in the form of new technologies, products and services. They have a lack of respect for individuality, and as a result, government today destroys people's initiative to take chances in business. It has run amuck."

He threw his hands up in exasperation.

He paused and started again, his face pallid, virtually expressionless, every word a heavy weight lifted and thrown.

"I spent the day amongst a pack of lawyers. I felt like they were gorging on me."

Joe rested his forehead on his hand. I had never seen him like this.

"I'm going to lose this place—my house."

Joe frowned at me and looked away. My stomach turned. It was not easy to see him like this.

"When?" I asked.

"Some time in October, or November."

It was another difficult pill. Somehow, Joe seemed okay with it all. Although, I had never known Joe to be a materialistic person, as he has never been showy or ostentatious around me, and if he was, it was only to entertain and ensure that everyone had a good time.

I was viscerally shaken by the startling things Joe said. He was not kidding. He was deadly serious. I told him I was sorry, that I couldn't imagine how difficult it must be.

It was Day 80 of the BP oil spill disaster. Sales at the Flora-Bama were considerably down. The community was still struggling and suffering. Everything was closing in on Joe.

"It has been a tough year. It's like global weirding…the BP Oil Spill, the Nashville floods, the media screwing us over with bad press, my financial challenges…I'm beginning to wonder when the pestilence and disease will settle in on us."

I chuckled. It was a weak attempt at sarcasm by Joe that hit awfully close to home.

There was a moment of silence. He looked at me.

"My options are limited," he explained. I can sell most of my Flora-Bama stock, but a lot of it will go to the Internal Revenue Service (IRS). I owe them a bundle in back taxes that I couldn't pay because the many deals I did went South. I certainly have challenges."

Joe paused and in a ten thousand yard stare looked off into the direction of the sinking summer sun. The marmalade marble began its precipitous dip below the horizon.

He began again, "I need to find a white knight—I need somebody who can come in and help me take care of some of these bad debts so I can save the Flora-Bama."

There was a clear uncertainty in his voice. He seemed so tired. I wondered if he would muster the courage, resolve and resources to save the amazing place he created, the venerable Flora-Bama.

On one of the many real estate deals Joe made he attached as collateral a portion of the parking lot at the Silver Moon package store. This arrangement gave his creditor's attorneys the right to go after the Flora-Bama Corporation. This was one of the bad debts that Joe spoke of needing to pay off. It was therefore critical that he find a benefactor, or white knight, as he no longer had the cash or assets to make the monthly debt payments he had made for several difficult years before the mighty crash. These were the same payments that had completely exhausted his once considerable personal wealth.

Chapter Eleven
Mr. Frank Brown

"Success is when a man gets what he wants.
Happiness is when a man wants what he's got."

-*Frank Brown, former long-time Flora-Bama night watchman*

The Flora-Bama is the lasting landmark it is today because of the tireless efforts of a number of hard-working, crafty and loyal people. Undoubtedly, one of these noteworthy individuals was Mr. Frank Brown, the long-revered, now-deceased overnight watchman of the Flora-Bama.

Many have attended the Frank Brown Songwriter's Festival in Perdido Key, Florida altogether unaware of who Mr. Frank Brown was. His story is as fascinating as the place he kept careful watch over for nearly thirty years.

Joe said he first met Mr. Frank in 1978, shortly after purchasing the Flora-Bama. He said that Mr. Frank was then in his late 70's, yet he was still emptying by himself steel drums full of trash that were kept on the side of the Flora-Bama compound. Joe said he couldn't believe Mr. Frank was able to lift these heavy metal barrels, much less the large amounts of trash they contained.

"You don't have to do this anymore," Joe matter-of-factly told him, and Mr. Frank thereafter concentrated mainly on what became his regular Flora-Bama evening security detail.

Joe said that Mr. Frank Brown was a noted prize fighter in Pensacola as a young man. In his youth Mr. Frank was reportedly a massive individual, evidenced by the fact that one of his clenched fists was nearly as large as both of Joe's closed fists.

"It was only one knuckle short," said Joe of Mr. Frank's gargantuan hands. "His single fist was almost as big as both of mine! Could you imagine being hit with that, with all of his might behind it?" Joe implored.

Joe added that Mr. Frank was for a short time in his young life a "Mule Boy." Joe said he asked Mr. Frank what being a Mule Boy was like. Joe said Mr. Frank replied, giving his best Mr. Frank expression. "They would tells me where they wants the mule and that's where I would puts him."

Joe explained that Mr. Frank told him that he also moved grand pianos, even when he was well into his sixties. He talked about the fact that Mr. Frank was a known gambler for some time, making rounds as a semi high-stakes poker player, obviously long before the game was available online, and had become such an accessible television commodity.

Joe explained. "Mr. Frank told me one time he was in a game where he was taking a lot of the players' money, and he could tell that they were getting mad because of it. A couple of the men even accused him of cheating.

He said Mr. Frank removed his billfold and handed one of the accusers a five dollar bill. Mr. Frank told the man to 'go buy a brand new deck of cards at the corner store,' and that he 'would beat him with that deck too.'"

Joe further explained that what the players did not and could not realize was that Mr. Frank had already sold the local store and many other area stores all of their cellophane-wrapped playing cards at a really low price--after he had opened each of the packs with steam, marked all of the cards to his liking, and re-wrapped them. Mr. Frank was apparently as cunning as he was strong and stout.

When he worked at the Line, Mr. Frank regularly wore a pair of matched working revolvers, slung low; but he of course never had to use them. Usually it was enough for him to simply say in his deep, grandfatherly voice, "Now, you boys don't have to be like that. What would yo' mamma say?" All the regulars knew and genuinely respected Mr. Frank Brown. He was as much a part of the Flora-Bama as any other person or thing during its inglorious past.

To his great credit, Mr. Frank didn't worry about material possessions. Mr. Frank often said, "Success is when a man gets what he wants, happiness is when a man wants what he's got."

Mr. Frank was at his best, just overseeing things at the Flora-Bama and listening to the music created by his musician friends. He was always the last person all musical performers saw at closing time.

Joe and Pat have spawned many fun activities and events at the Flora-Bama, but the Frank Brown Songwriter's Festival is particularly special to the

Flora-Bama community, Joe, and of course, the singers and the songwriters, as it honors and recognizes their songwriting craft. Joe explained, "We treat our songwriters with respect. It's the songwriters who create the magic and emotions."

The Frank Brown Songwriter's festival, started in 1984, is dedicated to the late Mr. Frank Brown, the revered night watchman at the Flora-Bama for 28 years, and whose moral values, integrity and strength of character still endure. "Mr. Frank," as he was known by all, who was 91 years old when he retired, was even once featured on radio legend Paul Harvey's syndicated radio show, "The Rest of the Story."

The Frank Brown International Songwriters' Festival was an idea born to honor Mr. Frank Brown through a gathering of the writers he so loved and admired. Today the festival provides an atmosphere to promote all writers, whether if they have written hit songs which made people open their eyes and view the world in a different way or whether they are aspiring writers and musicians who know they can do the same but simply need a forum in order to get their music out to the world.

Joe seems to always be at his best during the Songwriter's Festival. He can usually be found at the Flora-Bama and other local venues during those lively ten days, encouraging people to enjoy the many artists, but to also remember to be reverent, and quiet—so that the artists can sing and be heard. It's the one time of year that Joe asked people to tone down the noise, out of respect to the artists, as Songwriters' Festival is all about them.

Amazingly, Mr. Frank was 93 years old when he passed away in 1988. He left a legacy that everyone can share. Some say his spirit still lives on in the celebration of the music. Nevertheless, he certainly still lives on in the memories of those who were fortunate enough to have known him. These fond memories of Mr. Frank continue to drive and motivate the many talented hosts of the festival with his namesake. The atmosphere at the Flora-Bama during this time each year always inspires collaboration and teamwork among the business community. Although many of the participating songwriters are not household names, their songs are. The Frank Brown Songwriters' Festival has been aptly called "A living museum of songwriters and their songs." For anyone who loves singer-songwriters, the Frank Brown Songwriter's Festival in Perdido Key for ten days every November is for you.

Each year after 1984 the Festival slowly grew until 1996. During that year, so many songwriters sent their biographies for entry into the festival that many had to be disappointingly turned away. Over time, the good word spread throughout the country that the teeming Gulf Coast of Florida and Alabama was the place to be for songwriters to gather, collaborate, give birth to new music and enjoy the hospitality, inspiration and memories provided by the beautiful and inviting, Pleasure Island.

Still today, the mission of The Frank Brown International Songwriters' Festival is to continue to provide a stage for all types of music to be born. In addition, through the sponsorship of businesses large and small, the festival is a major contributor in the fall season, which is traditionally the area's slowest time of the year.

One of the annual goals of the festival is to bring songwriters into the classrooms to help expand our children's minds and creativity through music, for the children to see the person behind a song they know and love; for the children to know that they too have the capacity, the ability and the opportunity to enhance lives through their own words and music.

The songwriters even bring their music to nursing homes so the elderly know that there are truly people in the world who care about them. Music lifts the spirit, puts smiles on people's faces and brings back memories they had long forgotten. Each year the writers continue to bring their music to children who are hospitalized due to terminal illness to brighten their remaining days, helping them to briefly forget why they are there.

In short, the Frank Brown's Songwriter's Festival promotes the love of song and the unique joy and happiness it brings to the world. The festival continues to gain popularity as it regularly features Hall of Fame songwriters and some of the industry's best proven practitioners. As stated, you may not know their names, but you will certainly know their songs.

***

I caught up with Joe in late January 2011. By this time, a full year after we met, the news had broken about him managing to somehow save the Flora-Bama from the throes of his bankruptcy, although many of the particulars were unknown, at least to me.

Like he said he would, Joe lost his home on Old River in Perdido Key and was living with Bo Roberts and Chris Newbury at a house and property he still owned near the Naval Aviation Museum off Blue Angel Parkway, between Perdido Key and Pensacola.

I asked him how things were going.

"I've lost a lot of fur, but they haven't gotten any skin," Joe quipped.

I chuckled. "That's one positive way of looking at it," I told him.

"Well, I still have a lot of challenges ahead."

"Don't we all?" I added, taking a page out of his Socratic method teaching book.

"Yes indeed," he responded. Joe was noticeably much more upbeat, and I could tell that his outlook had improved, that the light at the end of the tunnel was no longer perceived as a runaway train. Although, I knew the challenges Joe talked about included finding a way to pay the many back taxes he still owed the Feds.

A few weeks later, during the spring of 2011, Joe revealed to me that he had indeed found the White Knight he was previously looking for—the person who could help him out of his difficult financial situation. He told me that this man John McInnis, and more specifically his son, John McInnis, III, were people that he had known for some time. He explained that the younger McInnis was partnering with him and Pat, and he said that he felt like in time it would be a good fit for everyone. He let on that he would tell me more about it later.

Days later, on April 28, 2011, Joe and I attended the private Jimmy Buffet concert tagged, "Night at the Museum," held at the United States Naval Aviation Museum. Only 500 tickets were sold for the event, and Joe was able to somehow get us tickets for the sold out museum fundraiser.

On the afternoon of the concert, as planned, I met Joe at his place off Blue Angel Parkway. Later, we were picked up in a small recreational bus by John McInnis and his son, John McInnis, III, his girlfriend at the time, Shelly Freeman (they are now engaged), and their driver.

Much of the story of Joe's new partners had been told to me by Flora-Bama regulars in the know, but it was good to finally here it from Joe, as well as to formally meet he and Pat's new business partner, as the deal cut with the McInnises made Joe and Pat minority owners. Further, moving forward, the younger McInnis, John, would be the principal.

That evening I was able to speak at length with both McInnises. Each felt fortunate to be able to help Joe out of the bankruptcy situation and to also help him and Pat move the business of the Flora-Bama forward with a much-needed influx of cash for facility improvements. They explained that their investment in the fabled institution was just getting started—that they planned to make it—with Joe and Pat's help, bigger and better than it ever was.

Per their deal, the McInnises helped Joe pay off the bad debts still collateralized by the Flora-Bama Corporation, meaning that the longtime beach bar was no longer in jeopardy under his bankruptcy proceedings. Nevertheless, Joe still had back taxes and other debts to worry about; but those challenges, according to him, would be there for some time.

Chapter Twelve

Having Fun: The Principle Business of Life

"This is the best life I've ever lived!"

-Joe Gilchrist

    How much fun can a person have? Can a human fully enjoy oneself by zealously pursuing worldly pleasures without feeling guilty for it? Have you too become so consumed with the rat race of life—of getting ahead for the sake of the attainment of wealth, rank or fame that you no longer enjoy yourself? Do you remember having fun as a child, and more importantly, its anxious anticipation? Is there any remaining fun in your life? Do you fully understand the concept of having fun?

    Do you ever enjoy a reflective period of early morning silence after a night of music, laughter and song well spent with friends? Do you still get excited at the prospect of carrying out well-laid plans for having fun? Are you ever slightly jealous of others who have much fun?

    Honestly answering these questions should get you thinking about your life and your personal pursuit of happiness. Often we must take inventory of our lives before we can realize where we are, and whether or not what we are doing is worthwhile. Like Joe says, you can always certainly become a lot more useless in life—and be much better off for it. He is right. Each of us should think carefully about what we truly want in life and then act accordingly to get it.

    There is a memoir in book form, written by Eilizabeth Gilbert, titled *Eat, Pray, Love*. The tome is about Elizabeth's year-long self-exploration on the Indonesian Island of Bali. It has also been made into a popular motion picture, starring actress Julia Roberts. In the story, Gilbert struggles with the oxymoronic Italian phrase, "Il bel far niente," or more specifically, its English translation, "The Beauty of Doing Nothing."

    This phrase is not unlike Joe's statement of "becoming a lot more useless in life." Perhaps we all just need to slow down and savor life, instead of rushing through it? Maybe we should try and fully taste things, rather than gulp them. Maybe we should more clearly see things and not blink past them. Maybe we should embrace our emotions and not ignore them for the sake of returning to our work—which sadly—sometimes prevents us from enjoying life.

The fact is that the accumulation of money and the things it can buy should not be the central motivating factor in our lives. You can actually simplify your life by limiting your possessions and live much freer; and become happier in the process. This however, is easier said than done, as it requires serious life changes to effect.

Most of the world's people live in underdeveloped countries. Few humans around the world enjoy the many creature comforts Americans do. In fact, most people in the world are penniless. Nevertheless, most of these people living in huts and shanties are happier than Americans. Why is this? Perhaps, because the best things in life truly are free? If this is so, working ourselves to death for the sake of material things seems in the least, counterproductive, and ultimately, altogether wasteful, in the grand scheme of life.

Certainly there is a happy balance between work and play. Each of us must find this balance in order to be truly happy. Joe Gilchrist has artfully helped clarify this novel concept of having fun in life. Through his work at the Flora-Bama he has tried to perfect this seemingly enigmatic pursuit.

"It has always been important to me to bring people together from all walks of life and every social stratum, and offer them an opportunity to meet other people, and of course, to enjoy themselves. I love people and one of my great pleasures is meeting people who are not like me, who come from a completely different culture than me. One of my most memorable experiences was when I went to Africa and I sat inside a mud hut and talked to the indigenous people of a remote village. It was such an interesting experience."

Joe continued.

"I would like to clarify that I'm not saying that you should have so much fun in your life that you become irresponsible. Everyone has responsibilities. However, if you can keep things under control and still engage in the activities that bring you enjoyment and fun—like kayaking, sailing, fishing, biking, hiking, walking, listening to live music, drinking responsibly with friends or whatever it may be that brings real pleasure to your life—then by all means do it. You may want to even try a few things you might not think are fun. They may just be. Live a little. God knows I have. I have no regrets. I've had more fun than most people—and I'm still trying. Like I've often said, it's the best life I've ever lived. But, it's my choice."

Blaise Pascal, the noted writer, physicist and inventor, recognized one of man's common shortcomings. He said, "We never keep to the present…we anticipate the future as if we found it too slow in coming…we almost never think of the present, and if we do think of it, it is only to see what light it throws on our plans for the future. The present is never our end…thus we never actually live, and since we are always planning how to be happy, it is inevitable that we should never be so."

Author, novelist, academic and essayist C.S. "Jack" Lewis, who wrote *The Chronicles of Narnia*, often said that nothing gave him more pleasure in life than spending idle, carefree times with friends, taking long walks, or engaging in good discussions. His philosophy on enjoying himself reminds me much of Joe Gilchrist's.

Lewis clarified this self-induced state of enjoyment, "My happiest hours are spent with three or four old friends in old clothes tramping together and putting up in small pubs—or else sitting up till the small hours in someone's college rooms, talking nonsense, poetry, theology, metaphysics…there's no sound I like better than…laughter."

George Sayer, a biographer who knew Lewis for thirty years, described him: "Jack Lewis was unusually cheerful and took an almost boyish delight in life… great fun…an extremely witty and amusing companion…considerate…more concerned with the welfare of his friends than with himself."

I would say these same things about Joe Gilchrist and his makeup and character. Another wonderful quality Joe has is his ability to make and keep friends. I believe, as do others, that humans share a profound longing for true, lasting friendships and the many benefits these symbiotic relationships can and do bring to our lives. Sadly, many Americans today don't know how to make friends, or are less-inclined to make them, because society has dictated through its commercial advertising that above all else, materialism—not healthy relationships, will bring them happiness.

However, when some people realize that they do not measure up financially or status-wise to what everyone says is adequate, it can hinder their well-being. Many of these people do not appreciate the unique things that make them valid, valued and interesting humans. Unfortunately, sometimes it is these same people who try to pretend to be something they are not so they can conform to what society demands. Sadly, they think material things will somehow bring them happiness.

Asking oneself "How can I be happier?" is an important question. According to a *Money Watch* article by Kimberly Weisul titled, "Scientifically Proven Ways to be Happier," researcher Jennifer L. Aaker, a marketing professor at Stanford University's School of Business, Melanie Rudd, a Stanford MBA student, Wharton marketing professor, Cassie Mogilner, and economist Richard A. Easterlin, have studied and written about humans and happiness, noting that inquiries into money and happiness have found surprisingly few correlations between the two independent factors. The three instead examined the manner people spend their time and how it affects their happiness. Their findings suggest that there are five guidelines anyone can use to increase their happiness. They follow.

Human Guidelines for Happiness

1. Spend time with the "right people." These are usually not people you work with, but people you tend to spend the most time with, like friends, family and romantic partners.

2. Spend time on "socially connecting" activities, such as volunteering and spending time with friends. Work is not 'socially connecting' and is generally one of the more unhappy parts of our day. Commuting also makes people unhappy. Volunteering is a good way to increase happiness. Forging happy memories is important, because it helps us isolate an event that happened in the past and extend its value into the future. Therefore, one way to choose experiences that will increase your happiness is to consider how you might remember them in the future. Remember to ask yourself: What are your happiest memories? How might you create more similar memories?

3. Day dream. The researchers call it enjoying the experience without spending the time. Research has shown that the part of the brain responsible for feeling pleasure can be activated simply by imagining something pleasurable. And we often enjoy the anticipation of something pleasurable more than the actual experience that we think is going to be so great. A common example of this effect is vacation planning. Some find it more pleasurable than the vacation itself.

4. Expand your time. How can we feel less rushed and hurried? Breathing slowly helps. In one study, subjects who were instructed to take long and slow breaths—versus short and quick ones— for five minutes, not only felt there

was more time available to get things done, but also perceived their day to be longer. Volunteering makes one feel like they have more time. Spending your time on someone else makes one feel like they have more spare time and that their future holds more possibilities. And finally, paying someone else to do the things you do not want to do can make us happier. Therefore, if you can afford it, hire someone to do a few obligatory tasks, such as cleaning the house, your yard or your auto. Then, use the time you've purchased, not to catch up on work, but to do something you truly enjoy.

5. Understand Aging and Happiness. Young people equate happiness with excitement, but as we age, happiness is more closely associated with peacefulness. Young people tend to get more happiness from spending time with interesting, new acquaintances, while older people get more enjoyment from spending time with close friends and family.

Although idyllic, it would be much easier if we were all friends to one another—if we allowed one another—and ourselves, to live and be happy in our own way. True friends accept people for how they are and who they are, and of course, do not judge. Joe has helped me to understand this important concept of living well—the everlasting importance and power of friendships. Joe has many friends, and because of this, he is and always will be an extremely fortunate and wealthy man.

Willie Nelson, in his book, *The Facts of Life and Other Dirty Jokes,* that I found at Joe's house among the many tomes comprising a crowded bookshelf, noted an experience he had from creating an impromptu concert out in the middle of nowhere in the State of Texas, bringing many different types of people together from all walks of life.

Willie stated in the popular book, "We are always afraid of the unknown. It's just natural. But once everyone saw everyone else, heard the music and baked in the sun all day, I think a healing took place. We learned that the same spirit lives in all of us. We are the same. There is no difference anywhere in the world. People are people. They laugh, cry, feel and love, and music seems to be the common denominator that brings us all together. Music cuts through all the boundaries and goes straight to the soul."

The omniscient Dalai Lama, when asked what surprised him most about humanity, answered, "Man. Because he sacrifices his health in order to make money. Then he sacrifices money to recuperate his health. And then he is so anxious about the future that he does not enjoy the present; the result being that he does not live in the present or the future; he lives as if he is never going to die, and then dies having never really lived."

Now, if that doesn't move you to reconsider your ways, nothing will. These considerations are sobering. Discover or rediscover what having fun means to you. Make time for it in your life and for your family. Plan for it. Work your plan. Enjoy yourself. One day you will be gone and it will be too late.

Remember Joe Gilchrist's wise words. "The principal business of life is to enjoy it. The sad thing is most of us do not realize it until it is too late."

Chapter Thirteen

Patriotism

"Un-American, adj. Wicked, intolerable, heathenish."

-Ambrose Bierce, the Devil's Dictionary, 1906.

Patriotism is the selfless devotion to one's country. Patriotism is important to Joe Gilchrist, and many other caring Americans who have lived well and prospered under the great promise of the American Dream. While patriotism may be construed by some as something reserved for Americans serving in the military, Joe simply sees serving others as part of our duty as being good citizens.

Joe has not forgotten the sacrifices made by our intrepid service people. He always tries to do his part to give back to them by participating in their continuing fundraising efforts at the nearby national treasure of the United States Naval Aviation Museum in Pensacola, Florida, which is open free to the public, and relies heavily on fundraising for regular programming, maintenance and upkeep. Further, Joe always tries to help our local armed service members by inviting them to the Flora-Bama for various events held in their honor.

Pensacola, Florida is referred to as the "Cradle of American Naval Aviation" for its pivotal role in developing the United States' Naval Air Forces. The area has produced some of the country's finest naval aviators. Its expansive Naval Air Base and attending thousands of service men and women comprise an integral, and certainly noticeable and respected part of the otherwise vibrant and relaxing beach destination and retirement community.

During our adventures together Joe brought me to several events sponsored at the Naval Aviation Museum and introduced me to two Marine Corps Generals—Lt. General Chuck Pittman, a former Deputy Chief of Staff for Aviation and General William "Spider" Nyland, a former assistant Commandant of the United States Marine Corps (second in charge of the United States Marine Corps). Both of these patriots are retired. Joe and I also saw a private Jimmy Buffet concert there benefiting the museum, held for only 500 lucky Parrotheads.

Joe regularly pays homage to our country's rich military history by taking part in the many fundraising and educational activities the museum regularly entertains on behalf of the open public. He always tries to support the museum's efforts, and because of his steadfast support, many of the administrators and Marine and Naval officers know him by look, name and deed.

In February 2002, just months after the September 11, 2001 terrorist attacks that killed nearly 3,000 unsuspecting Americans, Joe and a cadre of nearly 100 willing, patriotic gulf coast business owners and musicians visited New York City to show respect emotionally and financially to the burdened people of New York and to encourage support for tourism nationwide. The Flora-Bama contingent led by Joe dubbed the "Gulf Coast Loves New York Tour," viewed Ground Zero, the New York City fire stations, the Empire State Building and Central Park, as well as met with hundreds of the afflicted area's public servants.

While on that first New York trip Joe accepted an offer by the Nassau County Police Department to march in the St. Patrick's Day Parade. He went back a month later for the patriotic event and walked in the parade alongside Nassau County Police officers. He was invited by Jack Costello, the former Police Commissioner of Nassau County.

"There were millions of New Yorkers on the street," he recalled. "It was an incredible, emotional experience to march down the street and see all the respect the people gave to the policemen and the fire department people. I was lucky just to kind of march along with them."

In 2012, a decade later, Joe returned to New York City during the first week of February to commemorate the ten-year anniversary of the initial well-wishing trip. Regular Flora-Bama Musicians Chris Newbury, Reed Lightfoot, Bo Roberts, Grove Scrivenor, Buzz Kiefer and Mike Locklin performed at notable venues such as the historic Bitter End and Red Lion Inn on Bleecker Street.

The group also enjoyed a well-wishing trip to Harlem where they were entertained with music and eats by a contingent of veterans at the Colonel Charles Young VFW Post 398 located at 248 West 132nd Street between 7th and 8th Avenues. "Merging Manhattan Music With Southern Sounds" was the unofficial visit theme, as the group enjoyed Harlem performers Urica Rose, Seleno Clarke and his Harlem Groove Band.

"It is important to remember 9/11," said Charles Dupree, Post 398 Commander. "We're honored that these musicians would come all the way to Harlem to share this moment and their music with us."

Post 398 is named for Young, the third black graduate of West Point, who once rode a horse from Wilberforce, Ohio to Washington, D.C. to prove he was fit for command.

"I wanted people from the gulf coast to let people in New York know that everyone across the country appreciated how they stood tall after those attacks," Joe told *New York Daily News* reporter Clem Richardson.

"If you can ever combine the opportunity to enjoy life while you are doing something that's responsible and the right thing to do, then why not?" Joe told John Mullen of the *Fairhope Courier* in a January 27, 2012 article titled, "Flora-Bama Owner Reviving 'Gulf Coast Loves NYC trip.'"

Also worth noting is that Joe and his well-wishing contingent visited the famous Apollo Theatre in Harlem where they took pictures on stage and reminded the people of New York that the people of the Deep South appreciate them and the sacrifices they have had to make.

After Hurricane Katrina decimated the entire gulf coast region in 2005, Joe and his dear friend, Ed "Eddie Boy" Woerner, a local turf grass farmer/specialist and entrepreneur, drove four and a half hours to Canal Street in downtown New Orleans, Louisiana towing tons of cooking equipment and fresh produce and meat for cooking. Once on the scene, Eddie set up shop and proceeded to cook for hundreds of relief workers, fire, police and military personnel including the 82nd Airborne, serving the public in the disaster situation. Joe showed up later and assisted. Joe and Eddie did this on their own dime to help their fellow man.

"This is what patriotism is about—serving your country by serving your fellow countryman," Joe said.

It has been said that service is the rent we pay for living on this earth. Joe wholeheartedly agrees. He put his philanthropic, patriotic philosophy into quick perspective.

"I do not, and never will—but some people in America have forgotten the many sacrifices that have been made by past brave Americans in service of their country. It is important for us to remember that what we enjoy today in our country—our freedoms, our culture and our quality of life—can be attributed to the service of others. If we remember and understand that patriotically serving others is an important part of our way of life in America, then it should be encouraged and taught to younger Americans. Each of us in some way can and should help our country continue its great legacy."

Chapter 14

The Rise and Decline of the Redneck Riviera

"As condo prices fell, cautious buyers began to emerge. These folks, mostly from the Lower South, were much like their parents and grandparents who came to the coast in the 1950's and 1960's: white, middle class and comfortably so, but with just enough redneckery in them to help keep places like the Flora-Bama going strong forty-six years after it opened."

– *Harvey H. "Hardy" Jackson, III*

One of the many neat things about Joe Gilchrist is that because he knows so many people, you inevitably meet new people when you hang out with him. An old adage says that a man's wealth is best measured by the number of acquaintances and true friends he has. If this is indeed so, then Joe, is filthy rich, as he has met tens of thousands of people through the years in his role as innovator, proprietor and host at the Flora-Bama.

One afternoon at Joe's house on Old River during the summer of 2010, before he had to give it up to the banks who had lent him money and their attorneys, Joe said he wanted me to read an article about the Flora-Bama and the area. I had some time, and was always trying to soak up information on my subject, so I sat and received a thin paperback book Joe handed me. I forthwith sat in his large reclining leather chair with an ottoman and read the academic piece.

What Joe gave me was the spring issue of *Southern Cultures*, an excellent scholarly quarterly published by the Center for the Study of the American South at the University of North Carolina. It contained an essay titled "The Rise and Decline of the Redneck Riviera." The author of the piece is Henry H. "Hardy" Jackson III. His work so impressed me that I felt this book would be remiss without a chapter dedicated to it.

The 22-page essay is a colorful overview of the more salient points of a forthcoming book by Jackson bearing the same name and published by the

University of Georgia Press. The book will focus on the Gulf Coast area stretching from Gulf Shores, Alabama to Panama City, Florida since World War II; the essay focuses on much of the same, albeit it is not as in-depth as the book.

After I finished the piece and loudly declared my distinct approval of his work to Joe, he asked, "Would you like to talk to him? I have his number."

"Why not?" I answered, thinking it would be fun and informative to speak with him.

Joe called Hardy Jackson, a history professor at Jacksonville State University in Alabama. He can only be typified as a bona fide Southerner. He was a delightful fellow, and we briefly spoke. He encouraged me and I explained to him that I thoroughly enjoyed his work, and that it forced me to look at the Redneck Riviera from a different historical and cultural perspective, and that I would definitely include it in my book about the Flora-Bama and the surrounding area.

Jackson said in 1954, his grandmother bought property in Seagrove Beach, Florida. Two years later, she built a cottage there. The same cottage has been his family's home away from home at the beach for more than 50 years, and therefore he is familiar with the area casually referred to as the Redneck Riviera.

Jackson thinks the term Redneck Riviera first appeared in print in 1978, when Alabama native writer Howell Raines published a piece in *The New York Times* about how former University of Alabama and then-pro quarterbacks Richard Todd and Kenny Stabler creatively spent their off seasons on the Alabama and Florida gulf coast.

Jackson said that Raines narrowed his formal definition of Redneck Riviera to a small beach section beginning just west of Gulf Shores and continuing east to the Flora-Bama, "where 'Doing it at the line' was, and still is, taken as a challenge by many." He also mentions in the essay that you will find "Gulf Coast Riviera" references as early as 1941, when the United States Works Progress Administration Guide to Alabama was first published during the tenure of President Franklin Delano Roosevelt.

According to Jackson, "Raines' Redneck Riviera was a scattering of vacation cottages, honky-tonks, picturesque if seedy motels, shacks on pilings and cafes that served smoked mullet, presided over by sunburned, bearded, beer-soaked refugees from civilization, driving rusted-out pickup trucks. It was where people could say, as Kenny Stabler did, when a reporter asked if all the stories about him were true:

> "I live the way I want to live, and I don't give a damn if anybody likes it or not. I run hard as hell and I don't sleep. I'm just here for the beer."

Jackson claims that prior to the Second World War there were villages between Pass Christian, Mississippi and Panama City, Florida that "survived on fishing and a trickle of tourists from not too far away, vacationers who came down to spend a week or so in the few 'mom and pop' motor courts. They'd swim a little, fish a little, eat raw oysters, buy something tacky at a local shop, and some, freed from hometown social restraints, would visit local nightclubs, dance, drink and get rowdy."

According to Jackson, visitors to the Gulf Coast increased after World War II. The tourist economy grew during the roaring 1950's and "the season" from Memorial Day to Labor Day, soon became a "cash cow for locals." In a matter of years, upscale communities cropped up for those who wanted to retire along the beautiful Gulf of Mexico's Redneck Riviera.

"As the region grew up, so did the offspring of these early pioneers," Jackson explained. "Baby Boomers, the children of postwar passion, were part of the youth rebellion, with a Southern twist. Along with the Beatles and the Stones, they grooved to Lynyrd Skynyrd and the Allman Brothers. In the clubs they danced to the music they danced to at fraternity parties back in Tuscaloosa and Atlanta. Sometimes the bands were black, but the dancers were always white. These bourgeois Bubbas and Bubbettes created the Redneck Riviera that Howell Raines saw and described."

Jackson said that the family-focused gulf beach economy changed little until 1960. That was the year the movie *Where the Boys Are* was released in Hollywood, USA. The movie depicted a wild and raucous spring break in Fort Lauderdale, Florida. Before this movie, few Southern college-aged kids ever had a spring break. *Where the Boys Are* changed all that, and it became exceptionally cool thereafter for Southern college kids and even aging Southern Baby Boomers to hit the gulf beaches during the spring and early summer season. Beach towns on the gulf coast, according to Jackson, however, had to decide whether or not to take the windfall of tourism dollars coming from spring breakers or altogether forbid the overwhelming spring invasion hassle. Most, of course, took the money and tolerated the hassle—and a tradition was born.

Jackson further explained that through the 1980's and 1990's, the Redneck Riviera became increasingly more upscale, and refined. The success of non-traditional, new urbanist developments like nearby Seaside east of San Destin inspired others in the Deep South to build similarly, and according to Jackson, "…people who bought into that lifestyle were a far cry from those who bought into beach life three decades before. First with money from the hot stock market of the 1990's and then with low interest loans after the dot-com bubble burst, Baby Boomers began to buy into a gulf coast that a Baby Boomer generation of developers was developing to sell."

Harvey explained that the Alabama gulf strip of sand and surf was indeed the "Redneck Riviera stripped to its essence." *Sports Illustrated* writer Robert F. Jones visited and described the folks he found as falling into two categories, "upper-crust, matronly, Rotarian with cash register eyeballs, and the (Kenny) Stabler gang--raffish, sunburnt, hard of hand and piratical of glance."

I found the "cash register eyeballs" metaphor particularly telling and truthful. Most of us familiar with the Flora-Bama have seen these types repeatedly run through the area, as their avowed wealth and self-proclaimed status is as meaningless at the Flora-Bama as a lack of air conditioning and indoor plumbing.

Jackson continued, explaining how new money brought changes. "So it was that the Redneck Riviera, which had been slowly dying as Baby Boomers aged, became an investment opportunity for some, and a place of calculated and carefully controlled leisure for others. Meanwhile, more and more of the sort of people who had come down to make the region what it once was found themselves priced into a shrinking selection of motels and condos, and the bars and seafood joints they once frequented became in-vogue eateries with designer decor and ferns."

Jackson aptly detailed the hurricanes of recent years, chronicling the destructive descents of Frederic in 1979, Opal in 1995, Ivan in 2004, followed by Dennis and then Katrina shortly thereafter in 2005. He aptly explained how Hurricane Frederic was destructive, but more importantly, how it also opened up the entire Gulf Shores/Orange Beach area to condominium development, giving many of the Mom and Pop damaged beach home owners the final catalyst they needed to sell to the encroaching corporate condominium interests.

"Meanwhile, coastal folks were learning what is considered general knowledge today: That storms destroy, but that they also clear the ground for builders to build. Gulf Shores is a classic example. Before Frederic in 1979, Gulf Shores had only one chain motel, a couple of small condominiums, a few restaurants, bars and beach cottages. There was one bank and no supermarkets. The hurricane leveled most of it. Then came the easy credit of the 1980's. Banks had money to lend and Baby Boomers, now in their thirties and approaching their forties, were ready to borrow. Having learned to love the beach in their bourgeois Bubba days, they wanted to recapture the magic without having to sleep ten to a room—so they bought a piece of it."

These deadly and costly hurricanes were followed by the worst recession since the Great Depression. Collectively, the storms and the financial meltdown have irreparably changed things. Many of the speculation-driven, shining condo towers now sit vacant, a fateful reminder of the boom period that was replaced by an unprecedented bust. Further, the construction craze has effectively ended. Nevertheless, Jackson still thinks this unfortunate turn of events may actually help soon return the Redneck Riviera to its rightful, Rotarian roots.

Jackson explained, "As condo prices fell, cautious buyers began to emerge; people who were more interested in a vacation place that could generate a little money on the side than in a unit for quick sale and a quick profits. These folks, mostly from the Lower South, were much like their parents and grandparents who came to the coast in the 1940's and 1960's: white, middle class, and comfortable, but with just enough redneckery in them to help keep places like the Flora-Bama going strong. Though much of the old Redneck Riviera has declined and fallen dormant, from these seeds a new one may one day sprout and grow. There are those who hope so."

The Redneck Riviera has endured much in recent years—marking a definite low point in the natural ebb and flow of modern pleasure island events. While history has proven to repeat itself, one can only wonder what is in store for the Deep South's favorite summertime playground. Those who know and love it can only hope that it will endure and thrive—like the revered Flora-Bama, and our great country.

Chapter Fifteen

The Polar Bear Dip

"Time has a way of changing. It changes all the time."
-Mickey Newbury

On January 1, 2012, I finally participated in the last of the noted Flora-Bama calendar events that make the place a popular year-round spectacle of sun, fun and frolic. Ironically, it is the first on the calendar.

Polar bear dips are a fairly common occurrence in the Deep South. They happen in other states like Mississippi and Florida, and anywhere along the coast of the balmy Gulf of Mexico with its many tropical currents.

Joe and Pat, like modern-day versions of Tom Sawyer and Huckleberry Finn, have made a living of conjuring ways to attract new victims for their perpetuated, stated cause of having fun. The Polar Bear Dip may be their most impressive, planned, crowd-gathering event, as few establishments can attract thousands of thirsty New Year's morning revelers quite like the veritable Pump House on the Line. However, that has not stopped others from trying.

A new Polar Bear Dip happened in 2012, just down the beach, 18 miles to the west, when the Kiwanis Club of Gulf Shores ushered in its inaugural foray into local Polar Bear Dip history with their first New Year's Day dunk at the public beach at the "T" at the end of Alabama State Highway 59, right next to The Hangout.

On New Year's Day 2012, about 1,500 or so fun-seeking beauties and beasts clad in various types of bathing suits and water attire, as well as an assortment of zany costumes ranging from Papa Smurf to Marvel comic book super heroes, crowded the beach behind the Flora-Bama. There was even an overblown Sumo wrestler in attendance, along with many dogs in holiday costume. Pat McClellan's white Labrador, aptly named Bushwhacker, even made the run, dressed appropriately as a doggy reindeer. "Eat, drink, get wet and enjoy the live music," was the proverbial rule at the 27th annual Polar Bear Dip, which drew several hundred more casual observers than chilly gulf swimmers to the popular beach bar.

Most of the reveling throng got to the Flora-Bama around 10:00 a.m. for its early opening. The Bloody Mary was a popular early beverage choice, as was the mimosa, and of course, cold canned beer. I had a little of each, as I knew at noon I would have to make the inevitable plunge. I figured I needed antifreeze for the unlikely winter water dash.

January 1, 2012, turned out to be a fantastic day. Just before noon, under virtually clear skies, it was a lovely 72 degrees—and the water—a mere 60 degrees. Joe's faithful cohort and partner, Pat McClellan, a hulking presence in his swim trunks and muscle shirt, stood near the water's edge with a megaphone in hand. Next to him was a brightly painted banner spanned between two long wooden poles held by long-time friends of the Flora-Bama. It read, "2012 Polar Bear Dip, Washing Away 2011." Joe stood beside Pat, also clad in lively swim trunks and a frayed, fading Flora-Bama tee shirt.

Pat swayed backwards and pointed the megaphone straight up into the air. "Okay everyone, it's almost noon. We're almost ready for the plunge! We're gonna let Joe say a few words before we make the dip."

Pat handed the megaphone to a wide-eyed and bushy-tailed Joe, who assumed the identical, backward leaning posture as he pointed the megaphone toward the azure canopy above. Joe's voice boomed through the amplifying device.

"I want to thank all of you wonderful, crazy people for coming out here today to this charitable event. Thank you for taking time to enjoy what has become a great tradition here at the Flora-Bama. We're going to wash away 2011!"

Pat resumed possession of the megaphone from Joe and looked at his watch.

"Okay, we're ready to make the plunge! Here we go!"

He began the countdown.

"30, 29, 28, 27, 26, 25…"

The throng chattered with excitement as everyone crowded forward, assuming their own starting line posture, anxious to make the dash to the foamy turquoise water's edge.

"10, 9, 8, 7, 6, 5, 4, 3, 2…"

The log jam of scantily-clad, rambling revelers spilled into the powder white beach's chilly opal waters, creating a cacophony of shrieks and shrills that filled the unseasonably warm, ambient air.

The plunge was exhilarating. The cold grips you with an accompanying, powerful rush of endorphins, which many claim is great for the human immune system. In hindsight, there appeared to be many elderly participants, individuals who had obviously made the event an annual tradition, with many of their family and friends.

Since the outside air was so unusually warm, the milder water temperature and the diminished effect of the latent heat of cooling under bright blue skies made for an extremely pleasant 2012 Polar Bear Dip. Some of the old regulars told me that in previous years conditions were starkly different, remembering earlier Polar Bear Dip day temperatures ranging in the low forties under misty, cloudy gray skies. Instead, bathing conditions were ideal.

The Polar Bear Dip annually brings back many former dippers—three generations of them, and for apparently good reason, as the event is family-friendly. Put simply, it is good, clean fun! There was a jubilant, joyful, even youthful exuberance that punctuated the entire renaissance affair. For a few minutes everyone acted like children again—by doing something that most everyone else would have said was crazy—squealing, prancing, laughing and playing in the chilly gulf waters on New Year's Day, symbolically washing away all the worries and cares of the previous year, and of course, welcoming the inevitable new.

After the dip took place, the many hungry and thirsty polar bears lumbered back to the Flora-Bama to enjoy a free plate lunch of cabbage, black-eyed peas, pork and buttermilk cornbread under the tent outside where Jason Justice and his band Hung Jury made for a most entertaining backdrop.

I thoroughly enjoyed the 2012 Polar Bear Dip. Although the weather was most conducive, I look forward to doing it again with friends and family, regardless of the weather, as I felt like I really did wash away the previous year's cares, while simultaneously making way for the many untold adventures of the new. As a result, I felt mentally and physically ready to tackle another new year. I was excited, as I was motivated by the experience, and of course, a trip to the Flora-Bama is always as fun as it is meaningful!

***

On Friday evening, January 6, 2012, Joe and Connie Blum and I met in downtown Fairhope, Alabama at the Eastern Shore Arts Center, where the renowned artist, Nall, showcased a sampling of his fabulous work.

Joe and Nall both have ancestors from Troy, Alabama and have been friends for some time. After the event, we walked to Nall's studio nearby and viewed more of his spectacular art.

An apprentice of noted surrealist, Salvador Dali, who advised him to "Draw from life, draw, again and again," Nall is an eclectic practitioner, merging many mediums into tantalizing creations.

Nall is interesting and his art is as uniquely beautiful as he is multi-talented. I first discovered Nall from picking up a book on Joe's shelf at his former home on Old River. The full color tome, printed in 2000, conspicuously titled, *Alabama Art*, by *Black Belt Press*, is a compilation of 13 Nall-selected, Alabama artists. The book won the Mary Ellen Lopresti ARLIS/Southeast Publishing Award for "Best Art Book." I was moved by the highly visual book—so much so that I commented to Joe, "I would much like to meet this Nall character. I dig his art."

Joe answered that he and Nall were friends, and that I would likely get a chance to meet him, as they had past collaborated. Joe explained how he and Nall, back in 1999, when he was readying to unveil his museum and studio in Vence, France—a former 17th-century farm house acquired in 1986, from Jean Debuffet—worked together to throw a grand opening party—replete with Flora-Bama musicians.

According to Brucie Glassell, Joe's long-time friend and business associate who lives in Perdido Key, Joe's brother, David, and his wife, Jan, an interior decorator working in Birmingham, Alabama, were in Nice, France in 1999, having lunch with Nall; as one of Jan's clients was interested in a painting. Nall explained to the couple his grand opening plans for his new museum in Vence, and commented on how absolutely wonderful it would be if he could have musicians from the Redneck Riviera entertain his French Riviera guests.

David, in typical Gilchrist fashion, replied, "I can make that happen!"

Upon his return to Alabama, David spoke to Joe about Nall's wish. The dedication was set for July, so they had only six weeks to plan the rare intercontinental gig. Joe turned to a tried and trusted, iconic group of musicians and singers to make the trip. Rick Whaley, Larry T. Wilson, John Joiner—the trio known as "Southwind," and singer/songwriter Rock Kilough—were guys who could boast of playing the Flora-Bama every Saturday night for several years, since the crest of the high-riding mid 1990's.

Nall's plan was to have the musicians play for everyone at the Vence Town Square. Joe arrived in town a couple of days before the event and passed out dozens of Flora-Bama tee shirts. On the day of the event, there were French people wearing Flora-Bama tee shirts everywhere waiting to greet the fun-loving Alabama USA contingent.

Joe also got the Alabama Lieutenant Governor's Office to draft a proclamation—in French, commemorating the event. Before the musicians played, the proclamation was read to the crowd by Nall.

A few sentences into the reading, the crowd erupted into hysterical laughter. Apparently someone bungled the writing of the letter. Instead of thanking the people of Vence for inviting Alabamians to party with the mayor, it thanked them for inviting them to breast feed with the mayor.

After the snickers subsided, the entertainment began. "Sweet Home Alabama" was played for a most impressive crowd, which included Prince Albert of Monaco, various members of the French Royal Family, actress Candace Bergen, Ringo Starr, Alabama Governor Don Siegelman and other Alabama dignitaries.

Brucie said it was a heavily-costumed affair, with many interesting outfits. Joe wore a tuxedo that had been completely hand-painted by an artist. "He was a walking work of art," she said.

Once the music started, the champagne flowed liberally and Gucci shoes flew everywhere. The people wearing Flora-Bama tee shirts danced wildly, as they rarely ever heard such music in France. By all accounts, the concert was a roaring success.

In between sets, Flora-Bama musician Rick Whaley was part of a wild coincidence. While enjoying a cigarette off-stage, a bloke with a cig in hand approached him and asked for a light. Caught by surprise, Rick acknowledged the guy and realized it was Ringo Starr. Incredulous, he reached for his lighter—which just happened to be a Beatles lighter. He lit Ringo's perched cigarette.

After a couple of puffs, Starr commented "Well how about that! That's a nice lighter!" he laughed.

Brucie said that Joe's brother, David, may have had too much fun at Nall's party. She said at one point during the soiree he noted, "I can't work a room like Joe, but I get cooler by the glass." Minutes later, David strangely disappeared. After a cursory search of the area it was discovered that he inadvertently hit his head on an overhanging roof and knocked himself silly. Lucky for him, he fell and rolled harmlessly onto a flat ledge down a nearby hill, only six or seven feet below the overhang. Had he gone further, he could have easily fallen several hundred more feet, which would have proved fatal. However, David was summarily reclaimed by the reveling throng and returned to the party where, to his credit—he got even cooler.

The musicians who performed that day went on to play a couple more gigs on the French Riviera before flying back to the Flora-Bama via Pensacola, Florida. One of them, Rick Whaley—the guy who gave Ringo Starr a much-needed light—contracted meningitis, which required medical attention. Joe saw to it that Rick made it home once he was fit for transport. Despite the lone setback, it was a huge success when the French Riviera, with the help of Nall and Joe Gilchrist—went Redneck for a day.

The grand opening in France was such a success that Nall agreed to help Joe host an event at the Flora-Bama a few months later. The black tie charitable auction and dinner for the American Heart Association, held at the Flora-Bama in 2000, was tabbed "Art for Heart," and it included Nall arriving at the state line on a Harley-Davidson motorcycle. Nall was the honored guest, as he donated his art for the auction.

Meeting the colorful Nall was a treat. It strongly reinforced the fact that Joe's friends are as various as they are many, which is as enviable as it is laudable.

Chapter Sixteen

An Analysis of Integrity of our Current Class of American Political Leadership

"Politicians make promises they can't keep;

Keep printin' money till they get in way too deep,

It's the same ole lesson that they never learn;

They're too busy workin' on their next term,

Politicians keep makin' fools outta you and me.

It's been that way since the get-go…

It's always been that way."

– *Billy Joe Shaver lyrics*

Many of the problems American society is battling today have come from the collective failures of our political leaders. Our politicians, through bad policy, have threatened our country's ruin.

America was not always what it is today. In earlier times, before the lobbyists, the big government bureaucrats and the greedy politicians imposed their will on an unsuspecting public busy trying to attain the American Dream, things were much more promising, and optimistic; particularly for young people.

Americans have difficulty comprehending why our country has experienced such a financial Armageddon at the hands of our politicians. Let us recap their transgressions leading to the fall, understanding well that in order to destroy a capitalist society, its wealth-producing markets should first be destroyed.

Banks work on a nearly foolproof business model. Principally, if they lend money to people who can and usually do pay their debts, and who have collateral, their risk is almost non-existent. However, under the Carter and Clinton Administrations, Congress enacted policy via the Community Reinvestment Act that forced banks to lend to individuals who had neither the ability nor a track record of making their necessary home mortgage payments. These were tagged as subprime, or NINJA (No Income, No Job, or Assets) loans.

The federal government also streamlined regulatory requirements for Community Reinvestment Act loans in 1995, permitting, and really pressuring banks to authorize such loans without the guarantee of traditional creditworthiness criteria, such as the size of the mortgage payment relative to income, savings history, and even income verification. Instead, the Federal Government told banks that simple participation in a credit counseling program, many of which were federally funded, could be used as verifiable proof of a low-income applicant's ability to make his or her mortgage payments. Put simply, federal bank regulators forced banks to make bad loans based on nonexistent credit standards.

The embattled Fannie Mae Foundation singled out one bank in particular as the role model for all other banks in America in terms of its commitment to CRA lending. By 2003, Countrywide, the nation's largest mortgage lender, committed to $600 billion in low-income or subprime loans. Today, Countrywide is essentially bankrupted, and has been merged with Bank of America.

Because of the cheap availability of home-buying credit, home buyers were many, and houses were accordingly priced artificially high. Most houses were simply not worth the selling price. When the payments on these mortgages—many of which were adjustable rate mortgages (ARM's), were not made, it resulted in an unprecedented glut of foreclosures, flooding the market with vacant properties, which in turn caused a valuation crash. Today, Americans' cumulative wealth, which in most cases is tied to their home values, is roughly a third of what it was prior to 2008. Moreover, home supply remains high; and demand conspicuously low.

In retrospect, real estate investors overextended. Joe was certainly one of these people. Untold profits from the endless flipping of vacation home and rental properties finally saw the end of their glamorous run.

With the real estate and stock markets in shambles, the economy, four years later, remains in a funk. Lacking confidence for good reason, Americans are no longer in a position to sign new mortgages. Further, many are trapped in their undervalued homes, upside down, unfortunate victims of a publicly-aided scam perpetuated by banks theretofore considered too big to fail, who were later bailed out by the same government. Unable to sell their devalued homes, many Americans have found great difficulty moving to find badly-needed new jobs for themselves or their family. Accordingly, home ownership is no longer an attractive aspect of the American Dream. Many would logically prefer to rent or lease.

While Congress and the Oval Office worked overtime to destroy the real estate market, it also had its sights set on exacting larger capitalist-killing measures, like enacting Universal Health Care and crippling the U.S. stock exchange; together these policies effectively thwarted America's wealth-growing capacity. These results can be traced to even more dreadful measures passed by our elected officials in Washington, D.C.

The Gramm–Leach–Bliley Act, which is also called the Financial Services Modernization Act of 1999, enacted November 12, 1999, was an act of the 106th United States Congress (1999–2001). It was signed into law by Democratic President Bill Clinton, and it repealed part of the Glass–Steagall Act of 1933, opening up the stock market for investment among banking companies, securities companies and insurance companies. This allowed large Wall Street investment banks, like Goldman Sachs, to legally consolidate with commercial banks, which allowed them into the home mortgage market.

Gramm–Leach–Bliley removed lender risk at the neighborhood branch level. The smaller banks and mortgage brokers sold these mortgages to large investment banks, which removed their risk and exposure. The investment banks packaged the mortgages into collateralized debt obligations (CDOs). Investment banks turned around and sold these CDOs to investors. The investors consisted largely of pension funds and other retirement fund vehicles, which most Americans invested into.

The Glass–Steagall Act, passed in 1933, after the painful lessons of the Great Depression, formerly prohibited any one institution from acting as any combination of an investment bank, a commercial bank, and an insurance company, thereby limiting the risk any one of these firms could encumber on behalf of their clients. This was a consumer protection measure.

As stated, the Gramm–Leach–Bliley Act allowed commercial banks, investment banks, securities firms, and insurance companies to consolidate. For example, subsequent to the passage of the GLB, Citicorp, a commercial bank holding company, merged with Travelers Group, an insurance company, in 1998, to form the conglomerate Citigroup, a corporation combining banking, securities and insurance services under a house of brands that included Citibank, Smith Barney, Primerica, and Travelers. This combination, announced in 1998, would have violated the Glass–Steagall Act and the Bank Holding Company Act of 1956, by combining securities, insurance, and banking. The GLB was passed to legalize these mergers on a permanent basis.

GLB also repealed the Glass–Steagall Act's conflict of interest prohibitions "against simultaneous service by any officer, director, or employee of a securities firm as an officer, director, or employee of any member bank." With the passage of GLB, the stage was set for America's precipitous financial fall. Congress then deregulated the derivatives market.

The Commodity Futures Modernization Act of 2000 (CFMA), is United States federal legislation that officially ensured the deregulation of financial products known as over-the-counter derivatives. It was signed into law on December 21, 2000, by Democratic President Bill Clinton.

CFMA clarified the law so that most over-the-counter derivatives transactions between "sophisticated parties" would not be regulated as "futures" under the Commodity Exchange Act of 1936 (CEA) or as "securities" under the federal securities laws. Instead, the major dealers of those products (banks and securities firms) would continue to have their dealings in over-the-counter derivatives supervised by their federal regulators under general "safety and soundness" standards. The Commodity Futures Trading Commission's desire to have "Functional regulation" of the market was also rejected. Instead, the United States Commodity Futures Trading Commission, or CFTC, continued "entity-based supervision of over-the-counter derivatives dealers." These derivatives, especially the credit default swap, were at the root of the financial crisis of 2008 and the subsequent Great Recession that has crippled a once robust economy.

When CFMA was passed it opened up a galaxy of financial instruments which were basically unregulated. Credit default swaps, collateralized debt obligations, interest rate swaps—each of these are derivatives and all are totally unregulated. The SEC and CFTC are not looking into these questionable deals, so there is no way to prevent fraud occurring within any of it. And it is likely still occurring.

If all of these debilitating financial policy initiatives were not enough, America also fell victim to a most troubling, base emotion—one as old as man himself—greed.

Ponzi scheme rip-off artists Bernie Madoff and Allen Stanford along with Alabama-based fraudster Richard Scrushy, the former HealthSouth CEO who ordered the rehab giant's books cooked—and many other white collar criminals, helped destroy public confidence in the United States stock market. In hindsight, unchecked human greed on a massive scale fueled the entire financial malaise. Today's quickly changing morals and values have seemingly brought the entire world economy to its proverbial knees.

In 1806, Webster's Dictionary defined success as "being generous, prosperous, healthy and kind." Today, Webster's defines success as "the attainment of wealth, fame and rank." One can certainly see how attitudes and beliefs have changed across the world in just 200 years.

***

Joe Gilchrist and I talked much about the state of our country and its future prospects for success during this fast-changing time. Like always, Joe's comments and advice regarding politics were as matter-of-fact as they were heartfelt. However, with over thirty years of experience as an entrepreneur and business owner who has had to deal extensively with government, his credibility in this regard is unquestionable.

Going through old pictures from the Flora-Bama one day, I found an image of an aging sign hung outside the front of the establishment. It read, "We raise taxes for a living and sell whiskey as a sideline."

Being in business for over thirty years, Joe has had what can only be typified as a tenuous relationship with government.

"One of the saddest things to me, a real tragedy—is that young people don't realize the freedoms we have lost as a result of changes our government has made. These are freedoms they have never known, and likely never will.

"Both parties nationally have let us down; it's not a Democrat or Republican or a party thing.

"People have asked me how I ended up where I am financially. I like to say that 'I underestimated my already low opinion of the people making decisions in our government.'

Joe continued. "The Kondratieff Cycle, a theory put forth by Russian economist Nikolai Kondratieff in his 1925 book, *The Major Economic Cycles*, contends that the economy runs in measurable 50-60 year cycles representing high and low economic growth. These cycles are represented by three distinct periods: Growth, stagnation and recession, with some disturbing government factor causing the financial collapse. In essence, government intervention in the free market creates the business cycle. Unfortunately, every 50 or 60 years our government leaders, business leaders and individuals forget what the previous generations have learned—that government intervention in the market causes problems.

"To borrow a line from long-time Flora-Bama musician Jimmy Louis, there are unfortunately a bunch of "energy thieves" out there in American society who want to steal our country's momentum. These people do not realize how badly they hurt our country's progress.

"I believe that there are solutions to the financial problems our politicians have created. The job of our leaders is to find them. We the people need to elect intelligent leaders with character who will work diligently to solve the many problems facing our country. However, we must remember what Albert Einstein warned, 'The significant problems we face cannot be solved at the same level of thinking we were at when we created them.' In other words, we must give up what we were to become what we are not. We must change."

Chapter Seventeen

The Future of the Flora-Bama

"There are few beach bars left in Florida, because of development."

– *Joe Gilchrist*

The Flora-Bama has a new owner, John McInnis, III. John, who is 33, told me that he is glad that Joe and Pat stayed on as partners. He added that he would not have wanted to assume majority ownership of the Flora-Bama had Joe and Pat not agreed to stay involved with its regular guidance and operation.

Since Joe Gilchrist took over the Flora-Bama from the Tampary family in 1978, it has become a cherished local landmark, and as mentioned, he and his original business partner, Pat McClellan, have been successful in creating and holding a number of regular calendar events that have become local holidays, like the Polar Bear Dip, the Mullet Toss, and the Frank Brown Songwriters' Festival, among others. John, whose family has been successful in the road and bridge construction and debris removal businesses, sees no reason to alter this already successful formula for fun and frolic, which is certainly sweet music to the ears of local regulars and long-time patrons, who know well that tradition never graduates—especially at the Flora-Bama.

"I see the importance of the traditional Flora-Bama calendar events—like the Polar Bear Dip, the Mullet Toss and of course, the Songwriters' Festival in November. They are integral to the success of the Flora-Bama and its success over the past 40 years. Many of the events that have grown over the past four decades have followers that go three generations deep in some families. These are annual traditions that we will continue and only try to make better every year for our patrons," said McInnis.

John added that they have no plans to change any Flora-Bama events, and only want to improve upon them, if possible.

"An example of one that we will make better is the Flora-Bama Crawfish Boil. This is an event that is done several times throughout the year and is usually pulled off on a whim. In the past there has been no formal planning involved with it. We have been told that it normally just happens when everyone is in the mood for crawfish or when they are available. While that tradition will continue, we are going to start having a large Flora-Bama Crawfish Festival on the same date each year. Thousands will come to the event and it will become a new tradition that will hopefully thrive for another 40 years."

McInnis said there are even new traditions in the works. "We would love to make some of our events better and create some new ones. The only major new event we have planned is to not only have a few beach concerts throughout the summer, but to hold a Fall Music Festival that will feature music on the beach for several days. The best time of the year down here is September/October/November with regular sunny skies and temperatures in the 70's. Imagine how much fun it would be to spend a few days sitting on the beach listening to dozens of local and national bands. We want to make this happen on the beach behind the Flora-Bama."

The Flora-Bama is currently under a massive rebuilding project. It is experiencing another wave of structural improvements that will certainly alter its function and feel. McInnis explained the ongoing grand renovation plan with respect to what was taking place in early 2012, and what is planned for the future.

"Rebuilding the old bar and listening room that was destroyed by Hurricane Ivan is also important. It was a place where people from all walks of life gathered comfortably and spent time meeting new people and listening to great music. We want to recreate that environment. We are rebuilding the old bar room exactly like it was before, with the exception of making it a little wider to get two rows of tables in front of the stage. The pool room will also come back and will be larger than its former self. The only thing that will be dramatically different from the old building is that we are building two sets of indoor bathrooms—including sixteen new toilets for women, which is a change that we don't think even the most nostalgic Flora-Bama fan will argue with!"

McInnis said that they intend to retain and recreate as much as possible the Flora-Bama's tackily unrefined charm and appeal—that certain something that makes it as inviting as an old pair of jeans.

"Joe, Pat, and all the employees saved all of the old pictures and memorabilia from the old bar so everyone will feel like they are back in the old bar. We have a lot of the materials from the old building, including bricks, wood, the old main bar, mirrors, etc. All of those materials and ornaments will become a part of the new building. Although it will be new construction, it will seem as though it has been there since the early 1960's, and that is our intention. Other than that, we have no other plans outside of creating more parking slips for boats across the street and possibly adding some dock space."

McInnis also talked about his ultimate vision for the Flora-Bama. "My vision for the future of the Flora-Bama is simple. I want to keep it the way it has always been and protect it from 'progress,' which, as most of us have learned, isn't always good! People love the Flora-Bama because it never changes and we are ultra-sensitive to that."

"In many ways we feel that we can make the Flora-Bama better without changing it; and that is our goal. While I am an owner now, I am only one of millions who have been blessed to learn that the Flora-Bama is a special place where people from all walks of life, from all backgrounds, from all races, rich and poor, gather to meet each other and escape reality for a while. It is a place where people who would usually judge each other and avoid conversation let down their guards and meet people that they likely otherwise would not.

"As Joe Gilchrist has always told me, 'it is amazing to watch different people who would usually not socialize, meet each other and realize just how much they have in common.' The Flora-Bama is and always will be a place where people treat each other with respect. Also, the Flora-Bama represents the way life should be, and protecting that is what my ultimate vision for the place is."

Life is meant to be fun. Take it if you can—when you can. Toward this important end, there will always be a special place, nestled on the beautiful spot that is the Florida and Alabama State Line, where you can find it—good food, good music, good people, good drinks, good scenery, and good times—at America's Last Great Roadhouse—the loveable, irreplaceable, distinctly Southern, Flora-Bama Lounge & Package Store.

Epilogue

As it turned out, Connie Blum, Joe's assistant and friend, was right. She told me that spring afternoon in 2010, that I would, "never be the same again."

Without question, I am no longer like I was before this odyssey began. I am different, having spent more than two years observing the actions of Joe Gilchrist and all of the wonderful, talented and equally dedicated people who have embraced his vision and helped make his fabled landmark what it is today.

How am I different? I am much more aware of the importance of having fun in life. Toward this end, I fully understand it is important to plan for my and my family's fun. Further, I understand that planning to have fun requires thought and action on my part, and that if I do not have any fun, it is my own fault. And in regard to Joe's adage that we can always "become more useless" in life—I am sincerely working on it; although I doubt I will ever achieve the level of uselessness Joe so artfully embodies.

I am different in that I respect even more the dignity of other human beings, and that I more fully realize that we are all naturally different by design. I realize that each of us possesses something—a skill, a talent, a voice, a point of view or even an understanding, that is beneficial to the rest of us. We should look for this unique usefulness, or value, in everyone we meet.

I am more mindful of the difficulties musicians and songwriters endure to uphold their artistic pursuits. Further, I am a much bigger fan of live musical performances. I realize that most of these inventive people will never enjoy the financial success they crave and deserve, yet they are nevertheless happy to embrace the development of their talent despite the penury associated with it. These are beautiful, creative people. Without them, there would be no Flora-Bama. All of the great ones toiled in obscurity before they found their big break. Without the creative artists, the Flora-Bama would have folded long ago—another regular casualty of the unforgiving bar business.

I am more patriotic. Realizing that freedom is not free, that things in our country are changing seemingly for the worse every day, and that the future is never guaranteed, I understand even more the importance of being informed about current events and politics. I also understand that I can make a difference by having an educated, informed opinion, and by voicing it; thereby exercising my Constitutional right to free speech. And of course, I understand what Orange Beach resident and author Andy Andrews states in his book titled *How Do You Kill 11 Million People?* that it is important to vote and to participate in the democratic process; for us to fully vet our public officials with the use of the Internet and published voting records. Each of us can make a difference by practicing these public things in a private way.

And finally, I am more mindful of change, and how our country has changed; and continues to change. America's freedoms are in jeopardy, which only imperils opportunity, which further destroys hope, and with them, the motivation to work hard. Freedom, opportunity and hard work—they are three important things our country was built upon. They remain as crucial today as ever, as they are ingredients essential for the American Dream—that every American can seek opportunities born of freedoms and work hard to achieve their goals. These must continue if we are to preserve our grand democracy.

***

Joe Gilchrist has certainly been affected by all that has happened. Joe lost tens of millions of dollars of accumulated wealth, his former stellar business reputation, as well as his lucrative majority ownership in the Flora-Bama Corporation. However, despite the stinging losses, he has gained something even more valuable in the grand scheme of things—perspective.

"All I lost was money, and in the end, it doesn't really matter." Joe said. And he's right. Joe can now concentrate on continuing to have fun and promoting the once again—"New Flora-Bama."

Joe, like his initial partner, Pat McClellan, is now a minority owner; but he remains a steady, knowing influence on the operation he built as a brash young entrepreneur.

Interestingly, his financial troubles have allowed him to gain a new partner with resources—one willing to complete the post-Ivan rebuilding and the other renovations that were needed to bring the Flora-Bama completely forward as the nation's premier beach bar. Further, this arrangement has allowed him to somewhat embrace semi-retirement; but more importantly, it has allowed him to see how things might be without him—while he is still here.

So, while Joe has lost a bundle, he retained the thing that has made his and so many other lucky lives so much more enjoyable—the Flora-Bama Lounge and Package Store—a place that has somehow through the years survived a destructive fire on the eve of its opening, multiple hurricanes, an oil spill, a great recession and a bankruptcy.

Given its impressive run and recent grand renovation, the Flora-Bama is likely to easily last another half century, as in 2014 it will be 50. If the future operators of this fabled, landmark institution remember its storied history and the unique traditions that have made it an astonishing success under Joe Gilchrist and Pat McLellan, there is no reason to think it will ever close.

The responsibility inured to the next group of leaders of the Flora-Bama is not to be taken lightly. If money and power end up being their primary motivations, and results in a catastrophic diminishment of the character, fun and the quality of life that the Flora-Bama has represented for the Perdido Key community for nearly a half century, that what would indeed be a shameful legacy.

The End.

Afterword

I am grateful for both my brother, David, and Chris Warner, for the opportunity to discuss some of the fun events and moral lessons of my life. The Flora-Bama and the Old Town House in Pensacola were character magnets that have allowed me to meet everyone from con-artists and evangelists, to the most wonderful humans possible.

In my youth, as most people who are Ole Geezers like me, now recall, we had the freedom to walk through the woods, to ride bicycles across town or in our early teens, to take a boat by ourselves, and to find adventure. My brothers and our friends could fill two, six-gallon gas cans, jump in a boat and go from Bayou Chico to Navy Point and water ski. We met girls our age and went to Pensacola Beach and back. No licenses were required. However, you had to act responsibly and be home for supper. I'm sorry that most people no longer have the opportunity to feel that free when they are young.

The Flora-Bama is the second bar I managed. After teaching five years, which was a great period in my life, I managed the Town House Bar in Pensacola. That bar also brought many people together. That's where I first met a lawyer named Stanley Levin, who became a great music supporter. Stanley introduced me to a songwriter and artist I had never heard of. Mickey Newbury's music changed my life and 20 years later we became friends and partners in creating music. I also met Ken Lambert during this period. He is a wonderful character who has experienced life from nearly every imaginable perspective. Ken is now an ordained minister who is happier than ever. He achieved this happiness by helping others. Specifically, he visits prisons, jails and challenged people. He has been as great a friend as he is a gifted writer and humanitarian.

The Blue Angels Flight Team also visited the Old Town House Bar. These were guys like Bill "Burner" Beardsly, Kevin O'Mara, and a wonderful group of adventurous, fun, and special men who devoutly loved their country. Skip Unstead was also one of the Blues I especially enjoyed. Typically, most of the pilots would not discuss the challenges of flying, but one night Skip talked about a maneuver he did as one of the solo pilots. I don't think he would consider it a breach of trust, as much as it is by me an attempt toward conveying how challenging these men's lives are. Flying upside-down over a runway is difficult. If a plane loses speed for any of several reasons, a quick decision must be made. The pilot can flip the plane, dooming it to crash at an air show, and bailout. This is never a great option; or he can retract the flaps and landing gear and thrust for more speed to pull up before crashing. All this of course must be done while flying upside-down!

My old Auburn EAE fraternity brother, Jim Davenport was a Marine A-6 Intruder pilot in Vietnam. I can only imagine what it was like for him to dive on a target. He said that radar-guided guns at night sent fire straight at him. Jim realized that tracer rounds whizzed by his cockpit on the left and then the right. He said to me, "It makes you wonder where the other bullets went since only one in five shells is a tracer." Whew!

Trader Jon was a special character in my life and he certainly loved military men and women. I asked him one time how he met so many Admirals and Generals. He said "It's always best to meet them when they are Lieutenants or Ensigns."

I met Chappie James at Trader Jon's. He had not moved up as rapidly in rank as he should have, considering he was one of the famed "Tuskegee Airmen" during World War II. Jimmy Carter helped him get the rank he deserved. He became a four-star general and a fine Representative of Pensacola for many years.

By the way, Jimmy Carter, after his Presidency, once boarded a plane my brother, Lane and I were on. He went through the rows and introduced himself to everyone on the plane. I thought it was a classy gesture. I was able to tell him that I had met his mother, Lillian Carter, at Auburn. She was Housemother for the Kappa Alpha fraternity, and a wonderful character herself. She had her sons buy her a new Cadillac convertible, which she and the other housemothers drove around town. She also later joined the Peace Corps. She was a nice lady!

When I was a lifeguard in high school, at Bayview Park in Pensacola, I met a man with a barrel chest. He was in his sixties when he and I became friends. He told me that after being gassed during World War I, he was advised to rebuild his lungs by swimming. There are many stories that combat veterans cannot tell friends and family, because they are too horrible or painful for the veteran, or the audience. I remember the following war story every time I hear of a public servant or politician who takes a bribe or acts in their self-interest instead of what is best for his or her city, state or country.

World War I soldiers typically endured months of pain from rotting feet resulting from the wet trenches. They existed alongside rats and dismembered body parts of dead people. If this wasn't enough to destroy their sanity, a new enemy arrived—lice. The insects covered soldier's heads and other body parts and constantly made life miserable.

This former soldier told me that he and a buddy finally had all they could take and went out into "No-Man's land," risking death by sniper fire, to secure the body of an unknown, dead soldier that had been in the winter chill for three days—which was long enough to kill the lice and the eggs. They stripped the corpse, then stripped themselves and killed all the lice they could. After exchanging clothes, they said they were able to reduce their agony for weeks.

This story is one of many gruesome things that happen in war. The sad thing is that when men in every conflict make these enormous sacrifices to their health and sanity, it doesn't seem to resonate with some elected officials. How you can exist in this great nation and not do all that is possible to respect those who have sacrificed so much is beyond me. We are less as a society because of the poor actions of citizens, politicians and a restrictive government philosophy.

I am proud that both of my two brothers were Navy officers. I am also fortunate to have met so many young men and women who represent this county so well in the military. Thank you much—with all my heart! I hope we always honor your efforts.

When I was eight years old we lived in Pakersbury, West Virginia. My family visited friends with a son my age, and together we explored the riverbank, just as the spring floods began. While roaming the bank I fell into the river and clung to the edge long enough for my friend to save me. I sometimes think about how much fun I would have missed had I drowned. Not only that, but the tens of thousands of people who might not have met each other and tried to make the world a better place through music, fun and the nurtured, mutual respect for people, regardless of age, gender, economic and social status, ethnicity, etc. I often say "Young or old, rich or poor, we should all at least be nice to one another." I think often of Mr. Frank Brown, a wonderful man, when I recall what he would often say, "Now what would your mamas think if you act that way?" It always rekindles my love and respect for people.

I don't think anyone could make a better speech than Lou Gehrig's about being "The Luckiest Man," but I do realize how fortune has smiled upon me and the Flora-Bama. We have both suffered through storms, both physical and fiscal. I have made life-long friends like Billy Walker, Donnie Russell from Selma and "Eddie Boy" Woerner, who talked me into joining him in New Orleans after Katrina where we made a difference feeding the 82nd Airborne and the surviving members of the NOPD.

The number of military friends I have made is endless, but it includes one of my teachers at Pensacola High School, Mr. Bragg. He was one of the Marines in the 1st Marines at Guadal Canal. Through him I also met men of the 3rd, 4th, and 5th Marine Divisions, who spent an agonizing, soul-crunching 33 days in Iwo Jima.

Cook Cleeland was another character I met. He was a complex and fun man. He flew SBD Dive Bombers throughout World War II. The USS Wasp was sunk at Guadal Canal with him on board. There should someday be a book written about him. Before World War II, he was thrown out of the University of Missouri and then hitchhiked to South America! Then, without a passport or any money he hopped a freighter to New Orleans and jumped off the ship and swam ashore.

I respect people who can create emotion with words or music that other people can feel and share. I cannot list all of the wonderful people who I have met and heard. They are as varied as Ken Lambert, Jimmy Louis, J. Hawkins, Bo Roberts, Donna Slater, Leigh Anne Creswell, Larry Butler and many wonderful talents who have played at the Flora-Bama. I must include all the great writers and performers who have visited from time to time. I met Dean Dillon on the back deck at the Bama one day and we thought it would be great to run over to Kenny Stabler's house. A wonderful character, Kenny was still playing at Oakland then. Through Dean we started running into more singer songwriters. These were guys like Hank Cochran, "The Legend," Red Lane, who wrote 33 Haggard cuts, Mack "The Fireman" Vickery, and Wild Bill Emerson, who wrote "If heaven ain't a lot like Dixie I don't want to go." Willie Nelson, who I met several times, but he never visited the Flora-Bama, was a friend of Hank Cochran and Mickey Newbury. John Prine and Pete Fountain were other musical giants the Flora-Bama has seen.

Finally, thank you to Bo Roberts, who got Mickey Newbury to come down to play. Mickey said three days was all he would stay. It turned out to be a month! Larry Jon Wilson is another whose voice and music were legendary. I miss him and all of the wonderful friends who are no longer with us.

Thank you to Pat McLellan, my solid partner of many years and John McInnis, III for helping me to keep the Flora-Bama alive. I wish him great success and happiness in his important new role.

Finally, please take the time in your life to stay outside of small boundaries and to get to know people who are different from you. It is the best way to see how rich the opportunity of life truly is. Have fun vicariously with these stories. Perhaps I'll have time, in more than one way, to take on other adventures.

Like Hunter S. Thompson, I am also a "Gonzo writer." I have run out of time and am over deadline.

Thanks for the memories.

Joe Gilchrist
April 2012

Bibliography

Andrews, Andy. *How Do You Kill 11 Million People? Why The Truth Matters More Than You Think.* Copyright 2011 by Andy Andrews.

Baggett, Connie. "Baldwin cuts three highway jobs, awards equipment rental contracts." *Mobile Press-Register.* October 19, 2011.

Baggett, Connie. "Senator's Company Awarded $639,000 While he Supervised Grants for Boom Work." *Mobile Press-Register*, November 20, 2010.

Baggett, Connie. "Trip Pittman says boom work was legal, but he wouldn't do it again." *Mobile* Pres-Register, February 2, 2011.

Barker, Kim. "Spillionaires are the new rich after BP oil spill payouts." *Washington Post.* April 13, 2011.

Belt, Derek. "The last great American Roadhouse: Flora Bama offers musicians the opportunity to shine." *Mobile Press-Register.* June 24, 2007.

"Beyond the Beach: More than Just Sugar White Sand." *Decatur Living,* Late Summer 2011.

Browning, E.S. "Rapid Declines Rattle Even Optimists." *The Wall Street Journal,* June 14, 2010.

Busby, Guy. "Jimmy Buffet fans Assemble on Beach Hours Before Gulf Shores Concert's Start." *Mobile Press-Register,* July 11, 2010.

Busby, Guy. "Stephen Nodine may face murder prosecution, as Attorney General's Office takes over case." *Mobile Press-Register,* October 20, 2011.

Cheng, Jonathan and Lahart, Justin. "Economic Outlook Darkens." *The Wall Street Journal,* June 2, 2010.

Collington, Theresa. "Public Safety a Party Pooper at Flora-Bama." *WTSP.com* News Story (Tampa-St. Pete), January 2009.

Cooper, Peter. "Songwriter Larry Jon Wilson dies at 69." *The Tennessean.* June 21, 2010.

Cooper, Peter. "Larry Butler, Grammy-winning Producer, dies at 69." *The Tennessean.* January 20, 2012.

Curran, Eddie. "Given the Opportunity Stabler Would Erase tag 'Redneck Riviera'" *Mobile* Easterlin, Richard. "The Economics of Happiness." *American Academy of Arts and Sciences*, Daedalus Spring, 2004.

English, Antonya. "Flora-Bama Lounge is on the Border." *St. Petersburg Times,* St. Petersburg, Florida. September 29, 2007.

"Embattled BP Chief: 'I Want My Life Back'" *The Sunday Business Times Online,* May 31, 2010. Engler, John. "Drilling Moratorium is a Jobs Moratorium." *The Washington Times,* June 9, 2010.

Ferrara, David. "Fairhope Turns Senator Trip Pittman Spill Contract Records over to Federal Investigators." *Mobile Press-Register,* September 19, 2011.

Geiss, Chuck. "The Flora-Bama Lives On." *Black & White Magazine* Birmingham, Alabama, September 23, 2004.

Harding, Robin, Bond, S. and Mckenzie, M. "Jobs Data Stoke U.S. Recovery Fears." *Financial Times,* June 4, 2011.

Hazzard-Gordon, Katrina. Jookin'. *Temple University Press.* 1990.

Henderson, Russ. "Alabama Emergency Management Agency seeks documentation on how BP funds were spent." *Mobile Press-Register.* January 5, 2011.

Henderson, Russ. "Flora-Bama Lounge Owner Losing Two Properties in Groundhog Day Auction. *Mobile Press-Register.* January 24, 2011.

"Jimmy Buffet and CMT (Country Music Television) Present a Live Concert on the Gulf Coast." http://www.cmt.com/news/country-music/1642016/Jimmy-buffet, June 21, 2010.

Jumper, Kathy. "Alabama Gulf Coast condo developers say they can't afford promised bridge." *The Mobile Press-Register.* February 10, 2012.

Jumper, Kathy. "Flora-Bama in Perdido Key, Financially Troubled Landmark Lounge, gets a new Partner." *The Mobile Press-Register.* September 25, 2011.

Jumper, Kathy. "BP to pay developer $37.2 million to finish condo." *The Mobile Press-Register.* December 1, 2010.

Jumper, Kathy. "Chill out at Polar Bear Dips in Gulf Shores and Perdido Key." *The Mobile Press-Register.* December 29, 2011.

Jumper, Kathy. "Polar Bear Dips prove sunny in Gulf Shores and at Flora-Bama." *The Mobile-Press-Register.* January 2, 2012.

Langford, David L. "Get Down and Dirty on the Florida-Alabama Line." *The Associated Press,* April 9, 2001.

LaRocco, Lori Ann. "Joe Mason: The Gulf Drilling Moratorium is Costing US a Billion Dollars a Year." http://www.MSNBC.com, Thursday March 24, 2011.

Long, Margaret Childress. *The Best Place to Be: The History of Orange Beach.* 2007.

Lovely, Erika. "Obama Biggest Recipient of BP Cash." *Politico.com,* May 5, 2010.

Martin, Bob. "Riley exits office with a final trick: Aids political donors in $37 million BP recovery." *The Montgomery Independent.* January 20, 2011.

Mason, Joseph R., Ph.D. "The Economic Cost of a Moratorium on Offshore Oil and Gas Exploration to the Gulf Region." *Louisiana State University E.J. Ourso School of Business,* July 2010.

McClendon, Robert. "Senator Trip Pittman's company subpoenaed for oil spill contract documents." *Mobile Pres- Register*. October 7, 2011.

McClendon, Robert. "Where did the money go? BP gave Alabama $65 million in money for grants." *Mobile Press-Register*. November 22, 2010.

Mithen, Steven. The Singing Neanderthals: The Origins of Music, Language, Mind and Body. *Harvard Press*, October 31, 2007.

Moffett, Sebastian and Granitsas, Alkman. "European Crisis Deepens as Chaos Grips Greece." *The Wall Street Journal*, May 6, 2010.

Moon, Troy. "It's All About the Music." *Pensacola News Journal*, August 26, 2001.

Mullen, John. "Flora-Bama Owner Reviving 'Gulf Coast Loves NYC trip.'" *The Fairhope Courier*. January 27, 2012.

Nelson, Rex. "The Redneck Riviera." Southern Fried at http://www.Rexnelsonsouthernfried.com. October 15, 2011.

Nelson, Willie. *The Facts of Life and Other Dirty Jokes*. Random House, 2002.

Nolin, Robert. "Boca Plumber Claims Credit for Cap That Plugged Oil Leak." *Sun-Sentinel*. July 26, 2010.

Odom, Mike. "Federal Probe Began Last Year of Fairhope Contract to Alabama Senator's Company for oil Spill Cleanup." *The Fairhope Courier*. September 19, 2011.

Odom, Mike. "Senator Trip Pittman receives subpoena in federal investigation of BP oil spill contract." *The Fairhope Courier*. October 7, 2011.

Orndorff, Mary. "Former Alabama Governor Bob Riley registers in Washington as federal lobbyist." *The Birmingham News*. September 23, 2011.

Orndoff, Mary. "Former Alabama Governor Bob Riley trims federal lobbying client list." *The Birmingham News*. December 22, 2011.

Richardson, Clem. "Gulf Coast-NYC Bond Still Strong 10 Years After 9/11." *The New York Daily News*. February 2, 2012.

Robertson, Campbell & Lipton, Eric. "BP is Criticized Over Oil Spill, but U.S. Missed Chances to Act." *The New York Times*, April 30, 2010.

Rocker, John & Craig, Marshall. Scars & Strikes. RMC Publishing, 2011.

Rothbard, Murray N. "Kondratieff Cycle: Real or Fabricated" Sayre, Katherine. "Stephen Nodine facing new charges: criminally negligent homicide, perjury (updated)." *Mobile Press-Register*, Tuesday, August 23, 2011.

Sayre, Katherine. "Wilmer man accused of sexually abusing horse pleads not guilty." *Mobile Press-Register*. November 16, 2010.

Seitz-Wald, Alex. "BP Dispersant Toxic." http://www.thinkprogress.org/politics/2010/05/17/97408/BP-dispersant-toxic/May172010 Shaver, Billy Joe and Reagan, Brad. *Honky Tonk Hero*. University of Texas Press, Austin, 2005.

Simon, Rich. "Gulf Oil Spill: New Drilling Moratorium Issued." *Los Angeles Times*. July 12, 2010.

Steiner, Matt. "Springs Man's Claim to Have Obama's Records Starts Buzz." *The Colorado Springs Gazette*. March 29, 2011.

"Stressed Boat Captain Commits Suicide." *Los Angeles Times*, June 24, 2010. Strickland, Larry. Tales from the Davenport. *Trent's Prints*, Chumuckla, Florida. 2004.

Teske, Peter. "Wilmer man accused of sexually abusing mini horse waives preliminary hearing." *Lagniappe Mobile*. January 13, 2011.

Thompson, Michael. Former Baldwin County Administrator, Phone Interview. January 2011. "Thousands of BP Claims are Fraudulent, Says Claims Facility." http://nymag.com/daily/intel/2011/01thousands_of_bp_claims_are_all.htm. 1/27/2011.

Wallin, Merker, & Brown. *The Origins of Music*. Bradford Books, 2001.

Waxman, Henry. Letter to Tony Hayward. *United States House Energy and Commerce Committee*, June 14, 2010.

Weber, Harry R. "Cement Plug Permanently Stops Oil Spill." *The Washington Times*. September 19, 2010.

Weisul, Kimberly. "Scientifically Proven Ways to Be Happier." *Money Watch*, January 27, 2011.

Wernowsky, Kris. "Owner of Iconic Bar in the Red." *Pensacola News Journal*, March 11, 2010.

White, David. "Former Alabama Governor Bob Riley registers as lobbyist." *The Birmingham News*. August 10, 2011.

USA Today, Friday September 22, 1995 "Dixie's Rosy Riviera: The Boom's on at Alabama Beaches" York, Joe. "The Deadliest Throw: Inside the Mullet Toss—The Gulf Coast's Greatest Beach Party." *The New York Times*, April 6, 2011.

Ziemer, Joe. *Mickey Newbury*. Published by Joe Ziemer, 2004.